# THE STORY BEHIND AMERICA'S MOST CHARISMATIC AND CONTROVERSIAL PUBLIC FIGURE

Family man, Annapolis graduate, Vietnam combat hero, Oliver North has suddenly emerged as the most fascinating player in the Iran/Contra affair. Finding himself at the center of the most sensitive issue in America—aid to rebels fighting the Sandinista regime in Nicaragua at a time when Congress had refused such support—North has been outspoken in voicing his ideals.

Now, for the first time, here is the story behind the man, from his birth in a small upstate New York town, to his days at Annapolis and as a Marine hero in Vietnam, to his handling of the invasion of Grenada, the bombing of Libya and the capture of the *Achille Lauro* murderers, through his exploits involving Iran and Nicaragua.

*Defiant Patriot* offers a personal look at the most intriguing man in America today, tracing the rise and fall of the soldier President Reagan called "my favorite Marine."

D1636232

# DEFIANT PATRIOT

**The Life and Exploits of
Lt. Colonel Oliver L. North**

**PETER MEYER**

A MARTIN L. GROSS BOOK
ST. MARTIN'S PRESS/NEW YORK

Cover photo: Brad Markel/Gamma Liaison

DEFIANT PATRIOT

Copyright © 1987 by Peter Meyer

ISBN: 0-312-91091-6     Can. ISBN: 0-312-91092-4

Printed in the United States of America

First St. Martin's Press mass market edition/September 1987

10  9  8  7  6  5  4  3  2  1

**To Janet**

# Acknowledgments

This book would not have been possible without the assistance and cooperation of many people.

I am most indebted to the friends, associates, classmates, neighbors, collegues and acquaintances of Oliver North who gave of their time: Richard Allen, Charles Bolden, ret. Major General Edward Bronars, Lt. Col. Roger Charles, Linda Chavez, Edgar Chamorro, William Corson, Jim Coyne, Arturo Cruz, Jane Davis, Captain Michael De Haemer, Lt. Col. Ken Estes, David Evans, Roger Fontaine, John France, Denzil Garrison, Carney Giannatassio, Brigadier General John S. Grinalds, Joe Haag, Keith Haines, Rebecca Hamel, Commander Tom Hayes, Dr. Pete Hermance, Randy Herrod, Sam Hirsch, Lt. Col. Jack Holly, David Houghy, Mildred Johnson, Commander Al Katz, Jim Kiser, Lt. Col. Charles Krulak, Leo Kuehn, Rev. John Laboon, Michael Ledeen, Mark Legon, Brother William Martin, Greg Mathieson, Jim McNally, Donald Moore, Mark Newhart, Tom Parker, Dick Peer, Richard Petrino, Rob Pfeiffer, Helene Plotkin, Howard Rhodes, Major Greg Rixon, Russell Robertson, Evelyn Ronsani, Lt. Col. Dick Rusillo, Marta Sacasa, Peggy Say, Annette Shutts, Frank Simmons, John Sinclair, Coach Emerson Smith, Gene Stipe, Kathy Storm, Raymond Tanter, Jean Traver, Mark Treanor, Ernie

Tuten, Eric Van Dusen, Glenn and Vera Warner.

I am also grateful for the opportunity *Life* magazine offered me to help report a story on North and wish to thank my friends and collegues there, David Friend, Linda Gomez, Todd Brewster.

Other friends gave of their time and assistance in various ways: Annette Foglino, Terry Yahia, Stephen Soule, Marian and Andrew Drape.

My special thanks go to those without whom this book would not have been possible: John Drape, whose research and reporting dedication could never be properly rewarded, and my wife, Janet, who stood behind us all.

# CONTENTS

**DEFIANT PATRIOT**

"In the days ahead, only the very courageous will be able to take the hard and unpopular decisions necessary for our survival in the struggle with the powerful enemy. . . ."
—John Fitzgerald Kennedy
*Profiles in Courage*

# DEFIANT PATRIOT

*One*

---

# The Confrontation

THE LIEUTENANT COLONEL, HIS FACE SET IN A determined expression, suddenly broke into a smile as he threaded his way toward the witness table. His green Marine uniform, covered with seven rows of honors including the Silver Star, stood out prominently in the room of civilians—congressmen, senators, press men, cameramen, spectators.

On this morning of July 7, 1987, the world was focused on the Senate Caucus Room, a marble-columned chamber in the old Russell Senate Office Building on Constitution Avenue. The room had long been the stage for official American inquiries—from the investigation of the sinking of the *Titantic* in 1912 to the Watergate hearings that swept away a President.

Even before it opened, this segment of the Iran-Contra hearings had become the media event of the decade. The silent eyes of four television cameras followed the five-foot nine inch, well-proportioned Marine as he moved through the crowd, the space between his front teeth almost as conspicuous as his impressive Vietnam war decorations.

Several witnesses, including his former superior, National Security Advisor Robert McFarlane and the secretive, tight-voiced retired Air Force Major General Richard Secord, an operative in the tradition of fictional agents, had already appeared before the committee.

But television had been waiting for North. For the first time since the hearings had begun on May 5, 1987, the three networks were going "gavel-to-gavel," a coverage whose lost commercials would cost the media giants $10,000,000 a day. But no network could consider cutting this classic confrontation between the Congress and the man from the White House believed to have masterminded one of the most audacious covert operations in American history.

The media wasted no energy making this a historic communications event. Dan Rather of

CBS sat in a specially-built plexiglass bubble on the top of the Hall of States, the majesty of the Capitol Building, democracy's temple, in the background.

Only the luckiest members of the fourth estate had obtained seats for the session. In addition to the three networks, Cable News, C-Span, AP, UPI, reporters from around the world, including *Agence France* and the *London Times*, crowded into the room. The confused Soviet representatives of TASS, watched the proceedings on television.

The wire services were assigned two seats each at the long rows of table. The daily newspapers received only one seat, except for the powerful *Washington Post*, whose columnist Mary McGrory was given an extra seat at the request of committee chairman Daniel Inouye of Hawaii. Radio and television reporters were in a separate gallery, at the rear of the room.

When North arrived at the table to be greeted by his forty-three year-old attorney, Brendan Sullivan, he was also met by a blast of motor-driven Canons and Nikons wielded by the fifteen photographers fortunate enough to get assignments in the "pit," the shallow space between the witness table and the two-tiered dais where the twenty-six members of the Joint Committee on the Iran-Contra investigation sat, magisterially looking down on North.

It was designed as the best-engineered television spectacle in history. Even the table tops had been draped in red to provide color and cut down the glare of the polished wood beneath. The room's air conditioning had been augumented to handle the hot television lights and the usual muggy heat of the nation's capital in July.

The preparations were not in vain. As the hearing came to order at 9:00 A.M., it was estimated that some twenty-five million Americans were staring at the assured face of Colonel North, his dimple-cheeked, square-jawed smile seemingly indifferent to the fame—or infamy—that had already surrounded his name and exploits. Before his testimony was over, almost as many Americans had heard and seen him as usually vote in a presidential election.

Colonel North had come into this august room prejudged by many in the Congress and the media. To them he was a military man gone wrong, a battle-trained Marine imbued with power and heedless of the subtleties of democratic government. To the nation's cartoonists, he offered a field day—a "Rambo" incarnate, an Annapolis graduate who had risen to a pinnacle of power as an intimate adviser of the President, only to abuse that trust.

## The Confrontation

A camera sweep of the Joint Committee, ranging from the solemn faces of the congressmen to the cocky, almost sarcastic, grin of the long-haired counsel, John W. Nields, Jr., was revealing. It recorded their confidence that Colonel North was about to join the ranks of other remorseful members of the Executive Branch—men who were humiliated, even publically dishonored, by Congress. One of the prior witnesses, Robert McFarlane, had allegedly tried to kill himself.

The cocky young colonel would soon feel the same congressional sting, most were convinced. North had been too injured, personally and legally, to put up much of a defense. At the historic press conference on November 25, 1986, only days after the Iran-Contra connection was revealed, President Reagan had announced that North had been fired from his job as Deputy Director of Political-Military Affairs of the National Security Council. Attorney General Meese added that North was being investigated for "criminal" activity as well.

The mood was perfectly expressed by effusive ABC correspondent Sam Donaldson, who told the nation that Meese had charged North "with cooking up this scheme of skimming off money to send to the Contras."

North was accused of manipulating American

foreign policy all by himself, without authority from his superiors or the President. He was, as an unnamed White House source put it, a "loose cannon." In explaining North's culpability, Attorney General Meese told the press:

"The only person in the United States Government who knew precisely about this was Lieutenant Colonel North."

The young colonel was afraid of the truth, commentators insisted. As proof they offered the fact that on December 12, 1986, he had appeared before the House Intelligence Committee and taken "the Fifth," the hallmark of cowards. General Secord had already revealed that North had accepted a $12,000 security system for his suburban home in Great Falls, Virginia.

Even the appearance of Fawn Hall, North's beauteous and shapely secretary, had triggered rumors. The Marine was probably a wife-cheater as well, his critics trumpeted. The discovery that $2,200 in Contra traveler's checks had been cashed by him—one, suspiciously in a lingerie shop—only fueled the committee's cockiness. North might be a battlefield hero but in Washington he was a political tyro, sheep for congressional slaughter.

Another Watergate was in the making, most

congressmen and staffers smartly assured each other.

"We've taken all the fruit salad off North's uniform," a committee staffer boasted to a national magazine.

The special prosecutor, Lawrence A. Walsh, appointed by the President, had hired a staff of over one hundred, rented an entire floor of a Washington office building and begun handing out limited immunities to almost everyone except the obvious villain of the piece, Colonel North. The Tower Commission, which had issued its damaging report in February, asked the President, as commander in chief, to "order" Colonel North to testify without immunity.

The nation had gathered for the ultimate denouement—Ollie North was supposed to throw himself on his Annapolis sword. It was only a matter of minutes, the Joint Committee thought, before the jaunty Marine who had engineered the bombing of Libya, the invasion of Communist-controlled Grenada and the capture of the hijackers of the *Achille Lauro*, would join the other witnesses who now recognized the power of Congress—one increasingly denuding what had once been called the Imperial Presidency.

Some members of Congress had openly criticized North before the hearing began. Literary-minded Senator William Cohen of Maine spoke of "a portrait of Dorian *North*," an allusion to Oscar Wilde's *The Picture of Dorian Gray*, the tale of a dashing young man whose true self, a portrait, turned ugly and degenerate when his past caught up with him. Chairman Daniel Inouye had called North's behavior "stranger than fiction."

North's veracity was constantly challenged. "Lieutenant Colonel North's credibility is shaky as congressional investigators prepare to hear his story for the first time," one newspaper insisted. Justice Department attorney Charles Cooper testified to the committee that he wouldn't believe North's story even if he was under oath.

The legal and public relations deck seemed stacked against North. But those who knew him well were sure the fighting Marine would not easily accept defeat. "Ollie might have looked terrible during the training," says Annapolis boxing coach Emerson Smith, "but he never did the night of the match."

Outside of North's own circle, only those who had watched a rare television appearance on which Ollie North had appeared after his exit from the White House would know the truth:

"This Marine is never going to plead guilty to

anything, ever," Ollie reminded anyone out there who could hear his voice.

. . .

Oliver Laurence North now stood at attention, as he had been doing virtually all his life. He raised his right hand and took the oath. It was only a matter of seconds before the Congress and the veteran Marine came to blows, both legalistic and emotional.

North and his attorney, aggressive Brendan Sullivan, partner in the prestigious Washington criminal law firm of Williams and Connolly, had already shown their mettle in prehearing maneuvers. Despite the limited immunity North finally received from the special prosecutor, on June 18 the colonel flatly refused to appear before the committee in *private* pretestimony interviews.

His goal was simple: military surprise. North wanted to deny the committee the advance chance to hear what he would tell the nation. The Joint Committee could have held the colonel in contempt, but they didn't. Fearing a public relations defeat and a delay in North's testimony, they yielded to the persistent Marine. "They just kneeled," says Congressman Jack Brooks about his colleagues.

It was a harbinger of what was to come.

Contentious defense attorney Sullivan quickly took on the committee chairman, Inouye, himself a decorated World War II hero. He asked that North be allowed to read an opening statement—despite a committee rule that such statements have to be submitted forty-eight hours in advance. The senator turned down Sullivan's request.

"Here once again, the witness is asking us to bend the law and to suggest that he may be above the law," Inouye chided, apparently both fearful of North and gunning for his public hide.

With his rounded, horn-rimmed glasses, Sullivan looked more the wizened accountant than the brilliant defense attorney he was. He kept interrupting the chairman in a brash, brassy tone meant to irritate and gain attention. Even before the questioning began, Sullivan challenged the motives and fairness of the inquisitors.

"The thing that bothers me the most," Sullivan said in an outraged voice, "is to have listened over the last few many weeks when . . . false conclusions have been drawn, when members of this committee have said on national television that Colonel North is guilty, when members of this committee ridicule his assertion of his constitutional rights, when members of the committee suggest that when he appears, Mr. Chairman, he will not tell the truth."

Inouye tried to stop Sullivan, but failed, finally gaveling him into silence. It was a telling exchange, the first hint that Ollie North had no intention of succumbing.

Committee attorney John Nields, a nagging sarcasm permeating his voice and manner, finally asked North the first question of the day.

"Colonel North, you were involved in two operations of great significance to the people of this country, is that correct?"

"*At least* two, yes sir," North quickly corrected him.

In a subtle way, North was reminding everyone that many foreign policy victories—including the invasion of Grenada—had sprung from his office, Room 302 of the Old Executive Office Building just across from the White House, a record that had earned him the sobriquet by which he was known—Ronald Reagan's "favorite Marine."

Nields parried with a question that had made other witnesses cower with guilt.

"But these operations were designed to be secrets from the American people?" Nields asked, his thin voice rising.

It was a deceptively simple question, meant

to conjure up visions of high school civics and the glories of an "open" civilization. But to Marine North, experienced in fighting on both the battlefield and in the geopolitical arena, it was a chance to explain the difference between schoolroom theory and survival in the nuclear age.

"Mr. Nields," North responded, "I'm at a loss as to how we could announce it to the American people and not have the Soviets know about it."

Nields pressed, and North pressed back, comfortable in the arena of the Soviet-American contest.

"I think what is important, Mr. Nields, is that we somehow arrive at some kind of understanding right here and now as to what a covert operation is."

His manner was sincere and thoughtful, more like that of a teacher than a "hardnose" Marine.

"If we could find a way to insulate with a bubble over these hearings that are being broadcast in Moscow, and talk about covert operations to the American people without it getting into the hands of our adversaries, I'm sure we would do that."

Nields had wandered into the wrong pew: the fight against Communism. Congress, who had now set themselves up as North's enemy, had failed to vote aid to the Contras for several years, then had suddenly changed their minds. They had limited the production of MX missiles and other weapons and were constantly nicking away at the Reagan Doctrine of aggressive anti-Soviet action. In a way, North was standing tall for the President who had fired him.

The committee attorney, not sensing that he was in troubled waters, continued.

"In certain Communist countries, the government's activities are kept secret from the people," Nields said rhetorically. "But that's not the way we do things in America, is it?"

Colonel North smiled back, speaking over the heads of politicians to the television public outside.

"I think it is very important for the American people to understand that this is a dangerous world; that we live at risk and that this nation is at risk in a dangerous world," North said. "And that they ought not to be led to believe, as a consequence of these hearings, that this nation cannot or should not conduct covert operations. ... The effort to conduct these covert operations was made in such a way that our adversaries would not have knowledge of them, or we could deny American association with it, or the association of this government with those activities."

Ollie North paused. "And that," he added, "is not wrong."

The crackle of change was in the air. A once-dubious audience, expecting a stiff-backed rogue Marine, were now listening intently, electrified by North's zeal and by his confrontation with a Congress he thought more zealous in investigating executive branch mistakes than in protecting American security.

Nields moved quickly to change the subject, to the great unanswered dilemma: What did the President know?

The colonel responded immediately. He had never discussed the issue with President Reagan. But neither was he a "loose cannon" in the White House. He was a Marine who followed orders, on and off the battlefield.

"Throughout the conduct of my entire tenure at the National Security Council, I assumed the President was aware of what I was doing and had, through my superiors, approved it."

As North spoke, his voice became steadier and stronger and tinged with emotion. "I sought approval of my superiors for every one of my actions, and it is well-documented."

North continued, as if in minutes he could answer every accusation made against him during these slow, painful months.

"On or about Friday, November 21st, I asked Admiral Poindexter directly: 'Does the President know?' He told me he did not. And on

November 25, the day I was reassigned back to the United States Marine Corps for service, the President of the United States called me. In the course of that call, the President said to me words to the effect that 'I just didn't know.' "

North was not finished. "Those are the facts as I know them, Mr. Nields. I was glad that when you introduced this, you said that you wanted to hear the truth. I came here to tell you the truth—the good, the bad, and the ugly. I am here to tell it all, pleasant and unpleasant, and I am here to accept responsibility for what I did. I will not accept responsibility for *that which I did not do.*"

The hearing room quieted. The young Marine who had been cast out into the political cold by the White House only to be attacked by the Congress as if he were a proxy for the President, had captured the moment.

Senator Inouye broke the spell, gambling that he could defuse the power of this boyish-faced witness.

"Was that response from a written text?" Inouye asked.

"Those are from notes I made in preparation for this session, sir."

"It is not a verbatim written text?"

"No sir, it is not."

Inouye had lost and North had won. To his

straightforwardness, North had now added a reputation for eloquence.

Before the morning session of his first day's appearance was over, the public image of Lieutenant Colonel Oliver Laurence North had been transformed. From a shadowy operator in the supposed "basement of the White House," he had become a forthright young man desperately caught in a political vise between the executive and the legislative branches of government—a scapegoat of the system.

In those few moments, Ollie North—a defiant patriot—had taken America by storm.

*Two*

---

# Growing Up

ALTHOUGH HARDLY A TEXAN, OLIVER LAUrence North came into the world on October 7, 1943, in San Antonio. His father, brought up—as his son would be—in a rural upstate New York town, had come to Texas like millions of other young Americans, to train to fight the war against Hitler.

The robust boy was born to U.S. Army First Lieutenant Oliver Clay North and his wife, the former Ann Clancy. Dubbed "Larry," he was a true war baby. The United States had just invaded Italy in the mistaken false belief that it was the soft underbelly that would lead to Berlin; the Marines were soon to make another bloody, courageous landing to retake the Gilbert Islands from the Japanese. On the beaches of Devon in England, almost a million Americans were secretly practicing Overlord, the coming assault on Hitler's Atlantic Wall in Normandy.

Larry North's father was a small man, barely 5'7", and openly, enthusiastically patriotic. In 1937, he had graduated from the University of Pennsylvania, where he had been in the ROTC, and was commissioned a reserve officer in the U.S. Army. As if someone had anticipated Pearl Harbor, he was called up for active duty in November 1941, just weeks before the Japanese attack on Hawaii.

For the next six months, North was a transportation officer at Fort Ontario, New York, not far from his home in Philmont, a village of 1,500 about thirty miles from Troy. But soon after he married Ann Clancy from Oswego, he was transferred to Arkansas as a battalion training officer, then to San Antonio with a promotion to major.

By the time North was shipped off to Europe with the Ninety-fifth Infantry Division not long after D-Day, little Larry was ten months old. In Europe, as a supply officer in George Patton's Third Army, North fought his way into Germany. Surprised by a Nazi attack, he struggled under intense enemy fire to gather up weapons so his men could defend themselves.

He returned to Philmont after the war as a colonel, with a Silver Star for heroism. In the fall of 1945, the short, squarely-built soldier led the town's veterans parade down Main Street to the acclaim of the populace and the wonderment of his two year-old son, Larry.

The Norths had long been special in Philmont. The Ghent Wool Combing Company, one of the major employers in town, had been founded by Larry's grandfather. "Old Man North," as he was called, was the first of three generations to bear the same first name. He was Oliver North, called "Oliver." To avoid the label "Junior," his son, Oliver Clay North, was called "Clay." Young Oliver Laurence North was always "Larry."

The woolen mills, North's and others, dominated the village and its economy. The town had been prosperous for decades before World War II thanks to the surging waters of the Aguawamick Creek, which sent power through the giant spinning and winding machines that transformed oily raw bundles of sheared wool into miles of yarn. Three of the mills were right downtown, leaving little doubt as to what provided Philmont's livelihood.

The older North—Larry's grandfather—was

also a small man, and slight, some 120 pounds. Of Scotch ancestry, he had started in the "shoddy" business, the craft of buying and reprocessing used cloth. "He was so good he could take a variety of rags, mix them together and reweave them in such a way that you could get whatever color you wanted without dyeing it," recalls Joe Haag, who went to work for North in the 1930s when he was sixteen.

Oliver North had a reputation for honesty and meeting his obligations, a man of stolid beneficence. Arriving in Philmont in the 1930s after losing a mill in Troy to the great depression, North met his payrolls when other mill owners couldn't. "He always looked you straight in the eye, dealt with you directly and paid cash," says Haag.

Old Man North was often given credit for keeping the mills open, but the demise of the industry was being written large even as Larry's father, Clay, took over in the 1950s. A graduate of the Wharton School, he applied modern business methods, putting up a 30,000-square foot building to house the huge machines that combed the foreign matter out of the wool. But the proliferation of hydroelectric plants and cheap oil made the Aguawamick sluiceway expensive in contrast. He had even less control over cheap labor in the South—the Taiwan of its day—which was drawing the industry out of the traditional, but now costly, Northeast.

Little Larry did not grow up wealthy, or even particularly comfortable despite his father's prominent position in town. The family lived in a very modest two-story frame house on Maple Avenue, their life not unlike that of the families of millions of other returning veterans. Ike was President, and the chaos of war had receded, returning Philmont and the towns like it to their pleasant, traditional ways.

Clay was the first president of the Rotary Club and a member of the Board of Education. Ann North, Larry's mother, was a library trustee and active in the PTA. Larry's parents were both well-educated, intelligent people, but they had different backgrounds and temperaments. His mother, a tall, slender prematurely gray woman—perhaps two inches taller than Clay North—was Irish Catholic, with an open, gregarious personality, probably the origin of Ollie's pixieish nature. Ann came from a family of teachers. Larry's father was a disciplinarian and an Episcopalian, a strict Scotsman from a family of dedicated businessmen.

The Norths compromised on religion: the children would go to public instead of parochial school, but Clay would convert to Catholicism.

At Sunday Mass at the Church of the Sacred

Heart, they were an impressive family of six—the parents, Larry, his younger brothers John and Tim, and daughter Patricia. Clay, who didn't wear a tie at the mill, was usually attired in a suit and a double-breasted military trench-coat. Ann usually appeared with a striking hat on her silver hair. The children were dressed impeccably, with scrubbed faces. "If I had a family, I would want them to be just like the Norths," says long-time Philmont resident Jean Travers. "The kids were perfect. The parents couldn't have been better."

The only flaws in the perfect picture were small, if possibly significant. There were rumors that one of Larry's relatives had committed sui-cide, and that Clay North was excessively strict with his children, particularly with Larry. That plus Clay's daily—eventually futile—struggles to keep the mill going were the only vulnerabili-ties within an otherwise classic Norman Rock-well portrait.

Little Larry North was a village favorite: bright, friendly, good-natured, polite, and gen-erally obedient. Yet he possessed a streak of ad-venture and pranksterism that seemed paradoxical in such a mannerly child. Wedded to that was a face with a look of such innocence that some later commentators considered it cal-culated.

Even as an altar boy at the church parish, he attracted attention. "You know how an angel looks, well, that's how he looked," recalls Evelyn Ronsani, whose daughter received First Communion with Larry.

But in growing up, Larry—if not Huck Finn— was more Tom Sawyer than angel. Contemporary Dale Rowe remembers the time he and Larry North were at a birthday party and broke a lamp while showing off for their mutual heartthrob, Dotty Archer.

Larry once killed a snake and left it on the front walk of a neighbor who was terrified of reptiles. With cronies Dale Rowe, Pete Hermance and Billy Andrews, he bought fake vomit, whoopee cushions, ink spots and squirt guns at Carney's novelty store on Main Street. Duller days would bring them out to Table Rock to play war games. The same creek that ran the mills was a perfect summertime haunt. Up at the railroad bridge it was Larry who generally lept off first, shouting "Who's gonna come!" before splashing into the Aguawamick.

When he was twelve, Larry and a friend even experimented with forbidden cigarettes, burying them for the right moment in a mason jar in the woods near Table Rock. Neither boy had ever smoked, but Larry had watched his Dad and thought he should try it, at least once. They dug up the cigarettes and lit them, sputtering and coughing as the strange smoke traveled through their throats. The youngsters quickly tossed away the lit weeds and marched off. Fortunately, the forest floor was dry and the fire started immediately. The frightened boys piled dirt on the flames and raced away.

But despite Larry's pranksterish sense of fun, there was no doubt he was on a shorter leash than his friends. Larry was one of the few boys not permitted to "hang out" on the street corner outside of Palen's soda shop. He was kidded about the loud whistle his mother used to marshall the North children home. Larry rarely tarried once it blasted through the Philmont air.

The home regime was so strict that neighborhood youngsters joked that they could tell time by the North children taking out the garbage. One boy, anxious to waylay Larry, used the schedule to surprise him in ambush.

Convinced of the deviltry of idle hands, Clay North made sure his children were given regular tasks. They were never, at least not openly, out of line. The family seldom went on vacation and Larry worked a lot around the house, mowing the lawn, raking leaves—a job that still occupies him in his Great Falls, Virginia home.

Larry seemed to be an exact genetic cross of his parents. He shared his father's Scottish drive for work, and like his gregarious mother, had an Irish twinkle to engage the soul. "Larry was always a charmer," recalls Tom Gibbons, his high-school English teacher, an observation shared by millions who watched his congressional testimony. "He knew how to joke around, but never at anybody's else's expense."

Like many in his generation, he was "straight." A dedicated Boy Scout who sometimes came to school in his uniform, he absorbed the incantations of American patriotism from his father, from the Boy Scouts, from the local community, from his church. Unlike others, he wasn't an altar boy for only a year or two. He served Mass, often getting up at 5:30 A.M., from first grade through high school—winning an award from Sacred Heart. In high school, Larry, who was skilled in English and writing, won the contest for a patriotic essay to be delivered on Memorial Day.

"We had maybe thirty-five kids in our whole class in high school," recalls Eric Van Dusen, a good friend of North's. "And we were *all* straight in those days. In the middle of the fifties that's just the way we were."

The generation gap had yet to be discovered, and adults still maintained value-setting authority. Defying the establishment took on such tame dimensions as "Dress Down Day," a senior class protest in which the students came to school in shorts, sneakers and college sweat-shirts, in violation of the dress code. Despite his pranks, Larry was as straight as they came.

Larry's late father, who eventually lost his business in the 1960s and became a teacher at a local community college, was considered a dedicated and honest man. But he was also judged to be a dour Scotsman, aloof and de-manding. Despite the boy's work ethic, charm, and general obedience, any infraction of disci-pline reportedly upset the elder North.

When Larry was in the ninth grade, he was transferred out of the public school for an aca-demic year and sent—on a three-hour daily commute—to the Christian Brothers Academy in Albany, a school with a reputation for mili-tary training and strong discipline.

For most of his young years, Larry North was a happy, active high school youngster. Never a "brain," he was an above-average, competent student with a B average and an occasional A in English, and somewhat lower grades in mathe-matics, his weak subject. His reputation was as a "doer," a mover and shaker. At Ockawamick Central, he joined the school chorus, the chess club, the drama club, the student council, and the science club.

Although not a great athlete, he was as active

in school sports, joining both the track team and the cross-country squad. "Whatever you need, coach," was Larry's watchword, whether the request was to run the 100-yard-dash or carry the water pail.

"Sometimes we would go up against much bigger schools and by juggling my boys I could get a bit more out of the team," recalls former track coach Russ Robertson. "Larry would always do whatever I asked. 'If you think I can do it and you want me to do it, I'll give it my best,' is what he'd always say."

The coach, a former Marine, was invited in by the Norths for his counsel. Was a military career the right choice for Larry? As the eldest son of a former colonel, Larry was drawn to the idea, but he also understood the ideals of his mother and her family of teachers. He aspired to be an English teacher as well. At this juncture in his life, Larry North couldn't decide on his future.

"I don't think Larry had found himself in high school," recalls Annette Shutts, who had been his steady girlfriend for two years.

Larry was a popular youth, liked by both the boys and the girls, who thought him handsome and gentlemanly. In his senior year in 1961, he was not voted the "most likely to succeed" or the "brightest," but "the nicest-looking" and the "most courteous." Young North was always well-groomed, carrying a comb in his pocket to smooth back his thick, black hair. "When Larry walked into the room, you knew it," says his former English teacher, Thomas Gibbons. "He had an air of self-confidence."

That confidence helped gain him a job one summer as the caretaker at Mrs. Burley's Girls School, a private summer school near Philmont for daughters of the wealthy. "The girls just followed Larry around," says Gibbons, who taught there during his own vacation. "They were just waiting for him to run them over." Larry was the envy of the town boys because of his proximity to "Burley's Girls," who were off-limits to local young men. But Larry reportedly paid no romantic attention to the ladies.

Larry dated a few Philmont girls but his relationship with Annette Shutts was more serious. He took her on roller-skating dates in the high school gym, she remembers, and they dated at record hops and proms. "He was the first boy I ever loved," Shutts now says in recollection. "But we both had plans that didn't include serious involvement. We had things we wanted to do."

One of them, of course, was college.

· · ·

It is 215 miles, as the crow flies, from Philmont to Brockport, New York. With an early Canadian wind blowing off Lake Ontario, just a few miles to the north, it must have felt eons away for young Larry North. Almost eighteen in September of 1961, he had led a sheltered existence in Philmont and had never been away from home for any extended time.

Larry had won a State Regent's scholarship in his senior year of high school and what was then Brockport State College, just southwest of Rochester—a simple, inexpensive academic institution—became his newest goal. Rather than the military, he had settled on the tamer goal: he would become a teacher of English.

The flatlands of the lake region were considerably different from his home region, the lush hills of the Taconic range above the Hudson. Brockport was not a large step into the future, but it was a step. Besides, Philmont was becoming bleaker economically by the year. It was no longer a town for dreamers, as it was in the days of his grandfather. His father was desperately trying to save the family mill, but the town's milling days were almost over. Columbia County's entire industrial base, including the cement factories that sometimes left a neat coating of dust on cars, was beginning to fail.

Educational futures seemed brighter than entreprenurial ones.

Brockport College consisted of one, mostly brick, academic building with a churchlike spire. On the front lawn was a flagpole, passed daily by each of the one thousand students. Larry moved into Thompson dorm, a small two-story building that housed thirty students. Sophomore year he would be able to move off campus and share an old Victorian house, which classmate Glen Warner called "the kind you make funeral parlors out of."

It was an unimpressive environment, a place in which "you had to make your own fun," as Warner says. The college hangout in the center of the small town was "Higgins." A "big date" was dinner at the Rich House, where one could also partake of a few beers.

North majored in English, which suited his verbal, inquisitive, but still unfocused, intelligence. He earned good—generally B—grades in most things, but was unable to rise above a D in his advanced math classes. In sports, he favored individual competitions like cross-country running, cutting a solitary figure in the open spaces of upstate New York as the leaves turned and he ran miles in the cold. It toughened North and gave him time to think about his future.

The lure of the military and its disciplined

framework still had appeal for him. Like his father before him, Larry enrolled in an officers' training program, the Marine Platoon Leadership Corps, which ran a summer training program at Camp Lejeune, North Carolina.

That July and August, instead of sunning and swimming on the banks of Lake Ontario, or visiting his parents and friends in Philmont, nineteen-year-old Larry North crawled through the Carolina mud, learned to break down and clean an M-16 rifle. He absorbed the romantic legends of the "Shores of Tripoli," hitching his dreams to a quite unliterary star. He had fallen in love with the Marine Corps.

His military training that summer affected North strongly. In fact, Marine-to-be North was now more conscious of the indiscriminate use of firearms. Once, while standing with others on the edge of a running field, he suddenly bolted toward a far-off figure holding a rifle straight ahead. North startled the hunter by upraiding him for the way he was handling his gun. "I spent the summer watching films about what weapons can do," North told his friends. "That guy doesn't understand what he was doing, pointing his gun at people."

With his mind finally focused on his future— as a Marine rather than as a teacher—Larry pondered how best to advance that goal. He thought of the U.S. Naval Academy at Annapolis, where Marine career officers were trained.

By a touch of serendipity that can inalterably change one's life, and sometimes even history, North's schoolmate, Glen Warner, was quite familiar with Annapolis. In fact, his father was the soccer coach at the Academy.

"There are some guys you like and trust right away," says Warner, now a schoolteacher in Buffalo. "Larry was like that. When he told me he was interested in going to Annapolis, I said 'You ought to come down and look at it. I'll introduce you to my father.'"

Later that year, North made the car trip to the Academy with his friend, who introduced him to Warner senior, who in turn had Larry meet the cross-country coach. Back at Brockport, North immediately applied for Annapolis, receiving a New York congressional appointment to enter in 1963.

"He was the kind of guy who wanted the Academy and the Academy would want him," Warner comments.

Oliver Laurence North had found his vocation.

*Three*

---

# The Midshipman

THE GAP-TOOTHED, CREWCUT TEENAGER, looking like a casting director's model of an aspiring midshipman, let his eyes sweep the manicured expanse of the United States Naval Academy at Annapolis. It was a pleasant day in June of 1963, two months before his twentieth birthday, as he walked toward the swearing-in ceremony that would transform him from a civilian into a candidate for a naval—or Marine—career.

To the ruddy, slim-figured youth from the simple Hudson River Valley village, the sprawling 338-acre campus, or Yard, on the banks of the Severn River was an awesome sight that would always move him. The majesty of the setting, just blocks from the historic waterfront and equidistant from the wooden-domed Maryland Statehouse where George Washington had retired as commander in chief of the Continental Army, was overwhelming.

As Oliver "Larry" North moved with 1,800 other freshman midshipmen toward Tecumseh Court to take the oath of fealty to his nation and to John F. Kennedy, his commander in chief, he knew that he had a great deal to prepare for.

The previous October, the world had barely escaped nuclear disaster in the Cuban missile crisis. The President had successfully called on the U.S. Navy and the graduates of this very Academy to face down Nikita Khrushchev and his plan to make Cuba a launching site for missiles aimed at America.

On these grounds John Paul Jones was buried. Since 1845, when Secretary of State George Bancroft first opened the school's doors, thousands of Navy and Marine officers had graduated Annapolis. President Kennedy had delivered the commencement speech the previous spring, and the grounds had just been designated a national historic sight.

North—who was soon to be permanently dubbed "Ollie" by his Academy classmates—was older than most of the other plebes, many of whom had received their appointments at age seventeen or eighteen right out of high school. He had not made the trip to Annapolis either directly or smoothly. But his experience in the Marine training program at Brockport had reinforced his decision that his life ahead lay as a leatherneck. He had come to Annapolis the slow, hard way. But he was there.

The swearing-in site, Tecumseh Court—in front of Bancroft Hall, where Ollie would live with four thousand other midshipmen—epitomized Annapolis. The court's centerpiece was a large figurehead from the Civil War battleship *Delaware*, which had been scuttled in Norfolk harbor to escape capture by the Confederate Navy. The statue was actually that of a Delaware chief, but the midshipmen had named it after Tecumseh, a great warrior noted for his bravery.

To the plebes, the statue said it all: Courage and Excellence. Called "The God of 2.0," the lowest passing grade, Tecumseh supposedly rewarded—with academic salvation—anyone who could expertly toss a penny into his arrow quiver.

The first months at Annapolis were not easy, but young Ollie North displayed patience for the Academy's harsh obedience-building practice of hazing the new plebes. He had to endure not just the rough academic curriculum, which was no snap for academically middling North, but the constant harassment of upperclassmen as well.

They forced plebes to eat ice cream until they were almost comatose. Being rousted from sleep at any time of the night became as near routine as lights out. The hazing was designed to make boys into men. It *sometimes* succeeded, but it *always* made the plebes sore and weary.

At the core of the hazing was a 277 page, compact (3 by 5 inches) manual called the "Reef Book," a reference to the shoals that would destroy careless seamen. In it were the rules, history and organization of the Academy, the Navy, the Marines, everything from protocol to ship identification. The middies were also required to read the *Baltimore Sun*, the *Washington Post* and the school bulletin board each morning before mess. Ollie quickly learned that survival depended on memorizing all of it, to be ready for the devastating questions that would be leveled by what seemed to be sadistic upperclassmen.

For not knowing an answer, Ollie found that he had to perform athletically at a "Coming Around," as the obedience-building rituals were known. Failure to give a quick, accurate response meant a score of push-ups or a sudden half-mile run. "Plebe-hos" were mass indoctrinations in which first classmen (seniors) came into a room or hallway full of plebes, who quickly came to attention, chin in, eyes straight ahead. They were challenged with questions, the wrong answers bringing them to their knees for still more push-ups.

The "Reef Book" contained a strange passage for a military manual. It was one that Ollie has memorized to this day, one surely not far from his mind during the week-long congressional testimony.

Surprisingly, that Academy tradition is a passage from Shakespeare, specifically from Polonius' advice to Laertes in *Hamlet:*

*Be thou familiar, but by no means vulgar.*
*Those friends thou hast, and their adoption*
   *tried,*
*Grapple them to thy soul with hoops of steel;*
*But do not dull thy palm with entertainment*
*Of each new-hatch'd, unfledged comrade*
   *Beware . . .*
*This above all: to thine own self be true,*
*And it must follow, as the night the day,*
*Thou canst not then be false to any man.*

Those "friends thou hast" meant one's classmates, joined by a bond of friendship the Academy hoped would foster competition between the various years—whether Plebes, Youngsters (sophomores), Second Classmen (juniors), or the exalted seniors, the First Classmen. It was all part of the Annapolis plan for building loyalty and obedience, unwavering adherence to a chain of command from the bottom-rung seaman or mud-slogging Marine up to the commander in chief. It was a system that would one day help Ollie North challenge, perhaps even permanently change, history.

The rigors of the first months escalated as the midshipmen approached the halfway point, Hundreth Night, a day when plebes and seniors traded places. The "hazees" became the masters for a brief twenty-four hours. "We had been taking a lot of discipline because of it," recalls Ollie's classmate Tom Parker. "The seniors were being especially hard on the plebes, anticipating the tables being turned. We were bone tired."

Ollie and his pals had only one respite: the term break at Washington's Birthday, 1964, when they received a short leave, their first in six months. A car pool was quickly organized around five midshipmen, all with the same goal: Brockport, New York. Ollie had gone to college there, and it was the home of two other plebes. One of them was Ed Wagner, a second-year "turnback" who had failed one course and been forced to repeat the bone and mind-wearying first year.

The other was Tom Parker, also going home to visit his parents in Brockport. Wagner was bringing along two classmates from Texas, Michael Cathey from Garland and Bill Mullen of Dallas, who didn't have time to make it back there. Ollie was on his way to visit friends from Brockport school days.

The group rented a car, a new Chevy II, in Washington, D.C., thirty miles south of Annapolis and began the 400-mile trip. They had covered more than half the distance when, on that cold February night, Wagner was chosen to drive the final leg from Harrisburg, Pa. on. Because he was a "turnback" he had been spared the hazing. Ostensibly, he was the least exhausted of the group.

Wagner plowed through the night, listening to the radio news: the trial of Jack Ruby, who had killed John Kennedy's assassin, and the congressional hearings on Bobby Baker, former Secretary of the Senate and an LBJ buddy. Cathey was riding shotgun next to Wagner. In the rear, Tom Parker held the center. Bill Mullen was on his left, with Ollie North on his right.

Day had turned to night, and the weather worsened during the last fifty miles. Puffs of snow were visible as the temperature dropped, plummeting far below freezing. At least the car's defogger and heater were working. There was more radio news. The Beatles, an eccentric English singing group, had just gone home after mesmerizing young Americans.

But Wagner was more interested in world affairs, news about the Cold War that would shape his future. There was a report of the U.S. sending Polaris subs to bases in Spain. And another from Washington on Southeast Asia. The new President, Lyndon Johnson, was warning the Reds not to move any further in Vietnam. That hotspot was beginning to attract attention. In fact, 15,000 American troops, and some Navy units, had already been sent to fight in that unknown nation.

One by one, as the cold and the night closed in on the little Chevy II, Wagner's carmates dropped off to sleep. The time passed slowly for Wagner as he stared out at the white lines on Route 15 headed north. By midnight, Wagner was humming to himself, pushing to stay awake, crossing over into New York State with the snow now coming down in impenetrable sheets.

At 1:00 A.M. the Chevy passed the sign announcing an approaching junction, the little village of Painted Post, New York, about 120 miles from their destination. Everyone was asleep, even Midshipman Ed Wagner, the driver.

In the brief instant when the young driver's eyes nodded closed from fatigue, the unattended car swerved into the left lane, sideswiping the rear of an oncoming truck loaded with baled hay. The impact sent the Chevy spiraling madly forward, heading into the dark directly toward the oncoming traffic.

Wagner woke, but there was no time to regain control. The Chevy hit—head-on—an oncoming 18-wheel Mack truck trying to make a turn. The shock of the collision was so fierce that it crumpled the Chevy's front end like papier-mâché and even cracked the engine block of the giant Mack. The five midshipmen were tossed against the metal and glass interior of the car like so many rag dolls.

No one was buckled into their seat belts. Tom Parker's head smashed violently against the roof. Bill Mullen took the brunt of the crash against his back. Oliver North was heaved into the front seat, where Michael Cathey had managed to throw up his left arm just in time as he smashed into the car's dashboard. Ed Wagner was thrust forward like a rocket into the car's steering column.

Four of the midshipmen were lucky. This was the only time that Ollie North slept through a crisis, and it probably saved his life. "My dad always said it was because they were asleep that they weren't killed," recalls Marine Lieutenant Colonel Jack Holly, an Annapolis classmate now stationed in California, whose physician father was coincidentally one of those who treated Ollie at the Corning Hospital.

Ollie injured his back, broke his knees and fractured both his legs. But he lived. Parker sustained serious head injuries and would lie unconscious in an Elmira, New York hospital for three weeks. Mullen's back was badly injured. Cathey fractured his left arm and cracked some ribs. Only Ed Wagner, the driver, was unlucky. The impact instantly fractured his rib cage. The steering column crushed his internal organs, killing him almost instantly.

Watching his friend die was Oliver's first taste of death. "If he couldn't take that, the Marines weren't for him," Holly would later say. North was conscious and in pain as rescuers tried to sort through the wreckage at the Painted Post intersection five miles west of Corning, New York, to extricate the survivors. Ollie could hear his friends moaning. The smell of blood and gasoline filled the air.

It was almost 2:00 A.M. by the time North was pulled out of the frozen metal wreckage and taken to the Corning hospital, an old wooden structure in the center of town.

Glen and Vera Warner, old Brockport college friends who had driven Ollie to Annapolis when he first entered, were on their way to Buffalo when they heard the news on the radio. They immediately turned around and headed toward Corning.

"Tommy Parker had already been moved to an Elmira hospital because of his head injuries," recalls Vera Warner. "And they had Larry [Ollie] out on this hospital porch, which had been enclosed for the winter. The two boys from Texas were also there. It was a very cold day and it was cold on the ward. I remember thinking to myself: 'How can they get adequate care here?' "

Ollie stayed in that hospital for three weeks before being returned to the naval hospital at Annapolis for further surgery on his legs. It took Navy surgeons two operations to remove the injured cartilage from North's right knee.

The young plebe was lucky to be alive, Ollie was told by everyone. But in the faces of his doctors, Ollie read the more painful truth. He might never walk again, let alone return to Annapolis. His plans for a Marine career seemed dashed. But in the Annapolis hospital, Ollie showed the determination that had taken him that far. He asked visitors and staff to pray for him, even handing out medals of St. Jude, the patron saint of lost causes.

His overwhelming desire and the prayers of many apparently were not enough. After three months in the naval hospital, unable to attend classes, now barely able to walk, Ollie was forced to drop out of Annapolis. He was sent home to Maple Avenue in Philmont, telling skeptical doctors, nurses and classmates that he would be back next year.

The trip to the Hudson River Valley was a desolate one for Ollie, who had gotten a taste of the military life and had liked it. The hazing had been difficult, but he had survived, sensing that his age and spirit of cooperation had spared him the more ignoble humiliations meted out by upperclassmen. Besides, his intended career as a Marine would involve considerably more hardship than seniors could ever serve up at the Academy.

The seriousness of his dream of becoming a Marine officer was being echoed in the first headlines out of Vietnam. It was clear that in Southeast Asia the United States was slowly entering the only substantial military engagement since Korea, reasserting, as it had then, its right to protect a nation from Communism. Even the *Corning Leader*, in the same morning edition in which it reported Ollie's car crash, ran an editorial entitled "Why We Are in South Vietnam: Reasons Why U.S. Must Win." North knew that U.S. Marines, among the first troops dispatched to Vietnam, were already dying in combat.

But Ollie was leaving all that behind. At least that's what others thought. For him, the injuries were only the newest obstacles placed in the way of his career—injuries he would coax, cajole and force into repair. He would, he swore, will himself back to health.

The first impediment he discarded was his crutches, the symbol of his disability. Ollie gave them up, determined to walk at all times, no matter how painful. With no studies to occupy him and no upperclassmen to haze him, North concentrated on his legs. He pushed himself to the limit, exercising, walking, moving at all times. He walked only a hundred yards at first, then longer and longer distances. After a few months, he began to run, first slowly, then with all the strength he could muster.

To his former high school English teacher, the would-be-Marine promised: "I'm going to beat this."

Maple Avenue neighbor Howard Rhodes was there when Ollie was obsessively working at his pledge. One morning, North's mother visited the Rhodes.

"How's Ollie doing?" asked Rhodes, who believed North had only "a bleak chance" of returning to the Academy.

"Oh, he's working hard at building himself up," she answered. "He's probably jumping off the garage roof right now."

Ollie had designed his own crude prescription for rehabilitation, a young would-be-Marine's approximation of physical therapy, his bet that despite all odds, he would bring his bent legs back to Annapolis. Few people were betting on Ollie, but he was already developing the assured self-confidence that—somehow—a mystical destiny was guiding his life.

. . .

Seven months after the accident, in the fall of 1964, limping imperceptibly from the pins holding his fractured knee in place, Ollie North returned to the Yard on the Severn River, a plebe all over again. After a physical examination by shocked physicians, Ollie had been readmitted to the Academy.

"I was surprised they made Ollie a midshipman again," says Emerson Smith, the Academy boxing coach who had visited him in the hospital after the accident.

The physical standards of the Academy were

rigorous. No exceptions were made for plebe North. During his first days back at the Yard, Ollie had to run a mile and do his quota of pull-ups, push-ups and sit-ups despite his injured leg. He held back evidence of his pain and met the requirements.

"You don't get back into the Academy unless you've really got it," says classmate Al Katz, now a U.S. Navy commander. "They let a lot of guys go. But Ollie came back."

It wasn't only the physical demands that made Ollie's return tough. Repeating the plebe year meant leaving behind his most important affiliation—his class—to begin over again with new friends. "You started out with a bunch of guys and went through a lot together," recalls Tom Parker, who was also "turned back" because of the auto accident.

Class affiliation was vital as midshipmen climbed through school ranks just as they would in the actual Navy or Marine service. Competition between individuals and classes was stiff and ever-present. Every privilege was earned; every infraction of the rules had its penalty.

"I had a hard time fitting in when I was turned back," says Parker of his transition from the class of 1967 to that of '68, the same one made by Ollie. "I watched my friends who were now sophomores getting liberty on Saturday night, when our Saturday liberty ended at six P.M. It was hard."

Like it or not, North and Parker were now members of the class of 1968, which was to become a historic one. It was a class that entered the Academy the week of the passage of the Gulf of Tonkin Resolution—the de facto declaration of war in Vietnam—and ended at the time of the slaying of Robert F. Kennedy in a Los Angeles hotel. Like those of '42, '43, and '44, it was a war class. By the time of his sophomore year, it was clear to Ollie North that he was being trained for combat in Vietnam. As a Marine, he hoped.

There were 1,317 men in the class of 1968 that fall of 1964. Only 837 would graduate, and hundreds would serve in combat, either in the Navy or as Marines. Scores would be decorated or wounded. Five would die in action.

That fact came home to the midshipmen every day when they walked by the bulletin board in the Rotunda. "To Those Who Have Gone Before Us," it read. Underneath were the pictures of Navy men and Marines, all graduates of Annapolis, killed in Vietnam. By the end of 1965, when Ollie was in the middle of his sophomore year, more than 150,000 men had been sent to fight in Vietnam. By his junior year, the number was 365,000. The Tet Offensive, in which the Vietcong failed but which the media turned into a Communist "psychological victory," would come just six months before North would graduate from the Yard.

Every student was aware of Vietnam but the midshipmen were also remarkably isolated from the tensions tearing America apart. "We were incredibly isolated," Navy Commander Kendall Pease, president of Ollie's alumni class, told a reporter. "No television until the senior year, and very little free time. And to tell you the truth, we didn't really think about Vietnam. That's not to say we didn't discuss it, but the basic decision—whether or not to serve, to go— had already been made. It was a given. We'd chosen our careers and that was that. What did get to us was the board we walked by every day in the rotunda."

The class of 1968 was the reverse image of their peers on American campuses. While Ollie and his classmates were pledging allegiance to the flag, his contemporaries were saluting Sgt. Pepper's Lonely Hearts Club Band and vowing never to serve in Vietnam. While protestors were taking up the cause of Tom Hayden, Jane Fonda and Mario Savio, Ollie North was reaffirming his desire to become a Marine. The fact that the leathernecks were in the midst of a deadly ground war didn't weaken Ollie's resolve. The Academy was a center of patriotism in a nation slowly losing its pride, but even inside the confines of the Yard, Ollie North was considered a focused student and a staunch patriot.

"He made sure everyone knew that he wanted to become a Marine on graduation," recalls a classmate. North regaled the midshipmen with stories about the North Carolina Marine training camp he had attended while a student at Brockport. He still had his Marine uniform and showed his friends the correct way to fold it so that it wouldn't wrinkle in a seabag.

"For most guys, choosing where they want to go after graduation is something that starts happening in junior or senior year," recalls Richard Petrino, an Annapolis classmate. "With Ollie there was never any question. He was a Marine right from the beginning."

Midshipmen kidded Ollie: "If you ever get wounded in combat, you'll bleed green"—a reference to Marine Corps colors.

But those who knew North understood that his was not a simplistic military orientation. Ollie already sensed that there was more to modern warfare than the mastery of an M-16 rifle. Geopolitics, he became convinced, was the key to victory over Communism. All midshipmen were training for a Bachelor of Science degree in Naval Science, but they were allowed to elect one minor study as well. Oliver North chose International Relations.

North studied Latin American politics because he felt that the region was vulnerable to Communism. But no one, including North himself, could have predicted that twenty years later he would be testifying before the world, making that precise point.

But enthusiasm, patriotism, even a gradually developing intellect, were not enough to get Ollie into the Marine Corps. The car accident had left him physically scarred—under ordinary circumstances too injured to bear the rigors of Marine life. North had already demonstrated his resolve, and this was the last obstacle to his dream.

While his classmates slept, North rose every morning before reveille. North pushed himself beyond the expected. If everyone was commanded to run three miles, he'd do five. If fifty push-ups were the order of the day. Ollie did sixty. He joined the sailing team and the track team. His theory was simplistic, but apparently sound. If he pushed his injured body to the limit, and it performed well, he was no longer disabled.

In their senior year, Keith Haines, now head

of the Ollie North Defense Fund, organized a Christmas vacation flight for his classmates at Andrews Air Force Base near Washington. Ollie came charging through, seabag over his shoulder.

"What's the rush?" asked Haines. "You're just going to New York."

North smiled broadly, shaking his head in the negative. "Fort Benning, Georgia, Mr. Haines," North laughed, thrusting his arms out to simulate wings. Instead of going home, Ollie explained, he had arranged to go to jump school during the holiday.

Another rare vacation from the Annapolis grind was used as efficiently. As his yearbook entry would note: "Love of the luxuries of life took him [North] to Survival School in Nevada."

North was permitted to take this rigorous training, but the doctors were adamant on one point. No contact sports. Another injury could leave him crippled. But in his sophomore year, stunned classmates watched as Ollie grabbed shoulder pad, helmet and cleats and dashed out on the football field for the Academy's full-contact Turkey Bowl, a Thanksgiving tradition in which sophomores played the juniors.

On a chilly night in February 1967, Rocco Francis Marciano, former heavyweight champion of the world, climbed into the ring in front of two thousand cheering midshipmen in McDonough Hall. They had gathered for the annual brigade boxing championship match. Marciano, only the second boxer to have knocked out Joe Louis, was to be the referee.

His presence was a notable coup for Academy boxing coach Emerson Smith. Though not an intercollegiate sport, boxing had become a popular pastime at Annapolis with Smith's encouragement. It would become Ollie North's personal metaphor for victory. Despite Smith's warnings, North had joined the boxing team. "He had to struggle with that knee," Smith remembers, "but he never let on that it bothered him."

Tonight, Ollie would fight Jimmy Webb, a smooth pugilist and now the Secretary of the Navy, for the brigade 147-pound championship. Ollie was an underdog, but a capable one. Smith called him a "Friday night fighter" because of his knack of winning when it counted.

Though Ollie had won five pretournament bouts, Coach Smith made him obtain the doctor's permission to fight. North secured it, but during practice, he was decisively decked by a midshipman sparring partner. Smith felt he had only one choice: he sent North to sick bay and barred him from the tournament.

Ollie knew that he had to have a shot at the Academy championship in his weight class. Calling on his growing powers of persuasion, he convinced Coach Smith that it was only fair to let the doctors decide if he could fight. The doctors, too, relented. The match was made between the two midshipmen who would eventually become the most famous members of their class of '68.

The coach was now sure that Webb would trounce Ollie. "I watched Jimmy spar and he looked sensational," recalls Smith.

By the time Ollie and Webb climbed into the ring, battle lines had been drawn among the midshipmen. Rumor had it that Coach Smith favored Ollie. Because North was the underdog, he had given Ollie special attention in the days preceding the fight. Just before the two young men entered the ring, Smith leaned over to Webb. "Go a little easy around the head," he told the favorite. "You know, because of the accident."

"Even if that was nonsense," says a classmate who was in North's camp that night, "something like that would make you pull your punches a little. . . . I don't think there was any doubt that Coach Smith favored Ollie."

Smith doesn't concur, but he does admit: "I

always spent more time with the weaker guy, to make sure no one got hurt."

Ollie North was definitely the weaker guy. Jim Webb was a boyish, curly-haired middie of considerable strength. His boxing prowess dwarfed the reputation of "turnback" North.

Before the bell the two midshipmen limbered up as they were introduced. Like the other matches, this one would be three rounds of three minutes each. The applause was divided in the packed athletic hall, but as the bell clanged, the real cheering began.

North circled while Webb burrowed straight ahead. Both boxers led with their left shoulders down, Webb jabbing, weaving, jabbing again, looking impressive on his feet. North appeared to be sluggish, seeming to favor his bad knee, fending off the quick punches Webb was peppering him with—until midway through the round. Tapping his mouthpiece, North let loose a flurry of punches that sent Webb, more surprised than hurt, reeling. Ollie did it again, capturing some of the momentum Webb had built up. North's fans were cheering.

By the end of the round, almost everyone in McDonough Hall—except Ollie—was surprised that North was still on his feet. The second round was even closer. Webb had the skill and the power. Ollie had the determination. By the middle of the third round, both boxers had lost their form: the sweat rolled, the gloves pounded. Webb kept jabbing the less dexterous North, but Ollie kept bouncing back, searching for an opening.

Then suddenly, the match was over. The fighters moved back to their respective corners, where their gloves and helmets were stripped off. North had survived. That was a victory in itself. But a few minutes later, the judges had made their tallies and passed them to the student ring announcer.

"The winner," he blared over the loudspeaker, "and new bridage 147-pound champion—Oliver North!"

The victory had been tight, by a single point. But it was a miracle of sorts.

"Ollie led with his chin that night," recalls classmate Keith Haines, using an image that continues to characterize North. "He took his hits and kept coming back."

.   .   .

Haines, a 260-pound midshipman from Utah, was one of those who gained an early insight into Ollie's special determination. During the closing weeks of the first semester of the senior year, Haines was appointed "Bow-Wow," Battalion Officer of the Watch, responsible for coordinating information, duty and mail.

Like every senior, Haines was sweating out the final exam on thermal dynamics and fluid mechanics. The difference between an A and a B hung on just three of the thirty questions. An F meant you were out of the Academy. Haines was trying to study and sort out the battalion mail when he noticed a large envelope addressed to Midshipman Oliver North. It was from a correspondence school.

The envelope, Haines learned from Ollie, contained a test from a communications school in which North had enrolled by mail. "He could never get enough," Haines comments.

North was only an average student academically, graduating in the middle of his class. Much of his energy in his senior year went into pursuing his singular goal: assignment to the Marine Corps—the army of the Navy. There was a Marine quota: only one in six could sign up. Every year those slots were oversubscribed by eager Middies seeking the glory of "Montezuma," and getting selected was difficult. But as the dismal tolls of the dead and wounded among Marines trickled in from Vietnam, many in the Class of '68 tried to avoid ground warfare.

On January 23, 1968, a Navy ship, the U.S.S. *Pueblo,* was captured by North Koreans while on patrol, another reminder of the dangers that awaited their class. But sea duty was still tame compared to the dangers lurking in the Vietnam jungle. Many first classmen went looking for their black or brown shoes—black for ship duty and brown for air. Anything to avoid the *green* uniform of the Marine Corps. On selection night in March, when the seniors chose the service they hoped to join after graduation, the Marines did not fill their quota for the first time.

But that didn't include Ollie North, who was described by classmates as the "gungiest," "airborne" Marine Corps fanatic in the Yard.

Those who knew Ollie North as a devout Catholic are sure he did some praying as well. Father John Laboon, then the Catholic chaplain at Annapolis, remembers North as a religious person. "He came to Sunday Mass regularly and frequently attended daily Mass," Father Laboon recalls. "There was a seminarylike atmosphere at Annapolis, and young North was serious about his religion."

That same seriousness, even zeal, came through in his quest for a Marine officer's berth on graduation. It is illustrated by a story told by student brigade commander Richard Petrino. One night, after lights out, he spotted Ollie sidling through Bancroft Hall. Since it was final exam week, he thought little of North being up that late, but he inquired anyway.

"Ollie, what are you doing up? Studying?"

North shook his head. "No, I'm trying to get hold of my medical records."

Petrino didn't quite understand.

"I have to get into the Marine Corps," North replied.

"Anyone who knew Ollie knew exactly what he meant," says Petrino, who could have turned Ollie in. "I admired him. He wasn't breaking into an office. He wasn't hurting anyone. He just wanted to be a Marine."

This was an early indication that Oliver Laurence North saw rules as something, if not to be fully bent, at least to be massaged for maximum, practical efficiency. It's still not known whether he actually saw his medical record, but he was on a collision-proof course with the Marine Corps.

The best evidence that he was physically fit was his boxing championship, and his best supporter was coach Emerson Smith. Ollie decided to visit him at home.

"You know, Coach, Jimmy Webb is getting into the Marines," he reminded Smith. "If I beat him in the ring, that should be proof that I'm physically fit to make the Corps."

Ollie asked Smith if he had made a film of the

championship bout. Smith had. He retrieved it and gave it to North.

He lugged the film, a screen and movie projector and set them up in front of the Marine Corps Review Board. Pointing at the weaving image of Webb in the ring, Ollie stated confidently. "This fellow is getting a Marine commission. I beat him for the championship. I think that proves that I'm fit to be a Marine."

Smith recalls the anecdote with glee. "I'll be darned if he didn't talk them into it."

. . .

Older than most of his classmates by two years, at twenty-four Ollie North had assumed a mantle of leadership at Annapolis.

"Ollie was tough as nails, but he didn't wear it on his sleeve," recalls classmate Mark Treanor. "He didn't have an ounce of belligerence in him. He didn't have to kick sand in anyone's face to gain their respect."

North had the rare ability to command respect by his bearing and fairness, and his reputation for achieving what he wanted by seizing the unseen initiative. As he succeeded at each new goal, he gained confidence. His fellow upperclassmen also noted that he exacted his hazing tax on the freshman with greater generosity than some of the others. "He wasn't a fanatic like some guys who made you eat ice cream until you passed out from the cold," says a former plebe.

Before senior year, two midshipmen from each company were selected to be company leaders for the coming year. North was one of the two in his Seventh Company. By the fall term he was company commander, a role that was not unattractive to the young ladies in the Annapolis area.

"He was different from the other middies in many ways," says Kathy Storm, who met North on a blind date set up by a friend. "He knew exactly what he wanted out of life."

It was in Ollie's junior year, in 1967, that friends told Kathy they knew "a guy you ought to meet." Storm was then a speech therapist in the Ann Arundel County School system. She was disappointed when told her intended date was a midshipman. "Those I knew seemed very young," she says. "When they got together outside the Academy it was like a fraternity beer blast."

Her friends convinced her that North was more mature, that she should take a chance. On a quiet double date, dinner at her friend's apartment, she was impressed. "He had impeccable manners," she recalls. "He treated you like a lady."

The rest of the spring of '67, she and Ollie had an "adult" relationship, which meant dinner out instead of noisy beer blasts. Sometimes it was the Chesapeake Inn; other times, Mulmeister's, a local ice-cream parlor.

Like others who dated underclassmen, Storm usually picked Ollie up at the Yard in her car. She would turn the wheel over to him, and they would drive off. Occasionally, he rented a car or borrowed one from a friend. Only first classmen could own their own vehicles, "which was something you planned for years," says Richard Petrino.

Unlike some of the other women, she hadn't come to Annapolis seeking a Navy or Marine husband. "I ended up rooming with three girls whose boyfriends were midshipmen," she recalls. "And that wasn't unusual. Hometown sweethearts followed their boyfriends to Annapolis, and after June commissioning there were a hundred weddings—and that's only because they weren't allowed to get married earlier."

Storm wasn't a hometown sweetheart. That place in Ollie's life was taken by Lynore White, who had become his steady after his break with Annette Shutts. But White, a Smith College English major from Philmont, had already mailed Ollie's pin back to him after a lengthy correspondence in which she decided against the military life. It was all over by the time Storm arrived.

By the end of the spring, Ollie was dating her regularly, at least as often as his busy junior year schedule would permit. They enjoyed each other and spoke of everything, including marriage. Storm still had a hometown boyfriend in college in Youngstown, Ohio—a fact North was aware of—but she "really cared" about the midshipman. "He was totally forthright and honest," Storm says. "He didn't play games."

She accompanied him to the annual "Ring Dance" at the end of the school year, and the couple stood together, he in his dress blues and she in a white gown, under a horseshoe-shaped cavalcade of flowers.

But Storm was being pulled in the direction of her hometown boyfriend. At the Army–Navy football game that fall, only seven months before North was to be commissioned, she told him the news. "My boyfriend wants me to make a decision," she explained. "And I've decided to stay with him." Storm was not interested in becoming the wife of a military man either, particularly a Marine destined for combat in Vietnam.

"That means this will be our last date," North responded, preparing to turn his attention to his true love—his imminent career as a leatherneck.

. . .

His classmates called it "a muscle car." The Ford Motor Company, its manufacturer, called it a Cobra, a reference to the power of its 427-horsepower engine. Whatever, it was painted Marine Green after its new owner, First Classman Oliver Laurence North.

The car was just another expression of his zeal. That spring before graduation, he organized a premature trip to the Marine base at Quantico, Virginia, he and his Cobra leading the convoy on its sixty mile journey.

But his intensity soon turned back to another objective, a woman to replace Kathy Storm. In March of his final year at Annapolis, his cousin, Kathy Stenerin, gave him the name and phone number of a co-worker who was single and beautiful. The midshipman called Betsy Stuart.

At the time, Betsy, a recent graduate of Penn State who traces her ancestry to Confederate General Jeb Stuart, was a group sales manager for Hecht's department store in suburban Virginia.

In an interview with *Life*, Betsy related the beginnings of her courtship with "Larry".

When co-worker Stenerin first mentioned her cousin to Betsy, she said she wasn't interested in blind dates.

"He's going to the Naval Academy," said Kathy.

"Then he's too young," Betsy responded. She was twenty-four, actually the same age as North.

But when Betsy saw his photograph, she agreed to meet him. Over the next weeks, Ollie called Betsy regularly, but she was working long hours at the store. "Whenever he called, he got my roommate," she recalls. "And he was about to ask *her* out."

Their first date came in March 1968, when North arrived in his Cobra. Betsy was impressed by the first classman. She concluded that the handsome Yankee was not only "nice," but unbelievably dedicated.

Betsy quickly learned what this meant when North decided to skip his thirty day graduation leave and depart immediately for Marine officer training at Quantico, Virginia. "I guess he was afraid the war wasn't going to wait for him," says classmate Marine Lieutenant Colonel Jack Holly.

At Quantico, he even skipped weekend leave so he could inspect the terrain for mapping exercises. Not only was North afraid he would miss the war, he was worried he wouldn't be properly prepared to fight it.

As his courtship with Betsy developed, North became convinced that he had found a woman willing to tolerate his dedication to, or obsession with, the Marines and national service. One evening, he arrived at the apartment with a single rose in hand. Without a word, he presented it to Betsy, who was about to find a vase when she noticed a small ring attached to a leaf. It was a miniature replica of Ollie's Annapolis ring. They were, in the tradition of the Academy, engaged.

On November 13, 1968, only five months after he had graduated from the Academy, Marine Second Lieutenant Oliver Laurence North and Frances Elizabeth Stuart were married. The full Marine Corps ceremony was held in the Memorial Chapel at Quantico. North, crewcut and tan in his full dress blues and Betsy in a flowing gown and veil, stepped through an archway of sabers as they left the church.

The honeymoon was a prelude to the crises that seem to dominate North's life. The couple spent some time in Puerto Rico and called

Ollie's dad from Amarillo, Texas on their return to the States. Orders had come in, the senior North told them. Ollie was to arrive in San Diego in two days. North knew what that meant. He was on his way to Vietnam.

*Four*

---

# Vietnam

THE EIGHTEEN-YEAR-OLD CORPORAL PUSHED down into his foxhole between the tanks, listening to the silence encircle the night. In-country for only a month, he prayed that everything was all right, that the trip flares and claymore mines were set for this security detail on the flank of North Vietnamese territory.

He didn't even hear the first shell, which caught one of the tanks next to him. The impact blew him out of his hole and down the side of the hill. When he came to only a few seconds later, it seemed as if the world had exploded. RPGs—rocket propelled grenades—and small-arms fire were coming in from all directions, as if an entire battalion of NVAs were attacking the forty man platoon.

Fighting off the pain of shrapnel in his chest and leg, the lanky Marine from Oklahoma crawled slowly back to his foxhole. Inside, by the light of the flares, he could see that the machine gunner had been hit in the face.

Now numb, the corporal crawled in on top of the other man and took up his gun. No sooner had he opened fire than he saw his platoon lieutenant dashing across the field to his right. A mortar exploded almost on top of him.

The corporal immediately crawled out of his foxhole, enemy fire still raining down and grabbed his commanding officer by whatever scruff of battle fatigue he could grasp, then painfully dragged his limp body into the hole.

"I sort of threw him in on top of the gunner," Randy Herrod recalls of this hot July night in 1969. "And then I sat on both of them and kept firing."

He hadn't been firing long when he heard the familiar, demanding voice from below. "Get off!"

Herrod had learned to heed this man's orders. He jumped clear. The lieutenant, who only moments before seemed permanently out of action, was now pushing his way up and out of the foxhole. He didn't even thank Herrod but the corporal didn't mind.

"He just got up and started to direct the counteroffensive," remembers Herrod.

The battle continued for another three hours, the lieutenant ordering, urging his men on, at times fighting hand-to-hand with the North Vietnamese regulars who had overrun the thin perimeter the Americans had been able to establish. But when it was all over, the sun was rising over Quangtri in the northern sector of South Vietnam and the eastern perimeter of Leatherneck Square had held. Only six of the twenty-five Marines in the platoon were still able to fight. Randy Herrod was one of them. Another was the resolute lieutenant whose life Herrod had saved—Oliver North.

"He had eyes in back of his head," a company Sergeant told the press about Second Lieutenant Oliver Laurence North, Platoon Commander K Company, Third Battalion, Third Marine Regiment, Third Marine Division, I Corps.

This night a green recruit with the platoon for only a month had saved North's life. It proved what those who served with North in Vietnam knew about him: if he wasn't risking his life to save his men, they were risking theirs to save him.

In a war in which over 50,000 Americans

would die, North would be among the survivors. But he would feel the heavy frustration of a soldier who had acquitted himself and his men on the field, only to lose the war at home.

. . .

More than any single event in the past twenty-five years, the Vietnam War has shaped the life of the United States. And more than any other event, it was the one in which Oliver North grew to adulthood.

North shipped out to Vietnam in November, 1968, a period of the great national doubt. As the incoming president, Richard Nixon, was to say in a televised address to the nation: "North Vietnam cannot defeat or humiliate the United States. Only Americans can do that." And what Oliver North would see over the next year would be Americans at his side dying to preserve pride, while Americans ten thousand miles away demonstrated to frustrate it.

At Annapolis, he had four years to prepare for that moment: to serve his country in war. "He absolutely refused to let anyone outwork him," Marine classmate Jack Holly remarked in a recent interview. "He outresearches, outworks, outguts, and outfights you everytime."

The year North graduated Annapolis and

went to fight in Vietnam was a particularly onerous one for the United States. The Tet Offensive had begun at the end of January when 6,000 Marines were surrounded by 40,000 North Vietnamese and Vietcong troops at Khesan. Even after dropping more than 75,000 tons of explosives on the enemy outside the American-held fort—"the deadlist deluge of firepower ever unloaded on a tactical target in the history of warfare," according to author Stanley Karnow in *Vietnam: A History*—the United States quietly abandoned the outpost, taking out its troops, just as Ollie North was being commissioned a Marine.

In March of '68, Senator Eugene McCarthy, campaigning against the war, lost the Democratic primary in New Hampshire to Lyndon Johnson, but by only three hundred votes. On March 31, LBJ told the nation that events in Vietnam had defeated him and he would not be seeking another term as President. Five days later, Martin Luther King was assassinated, followed by the murder of presidential candidate Robert F. Kennedy on June 5.

While Oliver North was slogging his way through Marine training at Quantico, Virginia, in August of that year, Abbie Hoffman was fighting it out with police at the Democratic party convention in Chicago. The inevitable paralysis of national will created by such ideological conflict at home meant that Ollie North's war would be a very personal one.

There would be no national sharing of his and other soldiers' heroism. There would be no heroic ideal to come out of Vietnam. Only individual heroes. Like Ollie North.

. . .

On February 22, 1969, Second Lieutenant North was riding atop the lead tank directing a reconnaissance operation when his platoon was ambushed by a large North Vietnamese force hidden in the surrounding forest. He had been in the country less than three months, but his Marine boots were totally immersed in the blood of war.

"He's a natural leader. It comes out of his pores," says Father John Laboon, the Catholic chaplain at Annapolis and in Vietnam at the same times as Ollie. "He wasn't afraid of getting wounded in combat. He wasn't even afraid of getting killed."

North remained on the top of the tank, returning enemy fire and directing his men to cover until the turret suddenly swiveled about, sending him crashing to the ground. The

Bronze Star citation, which he received for that action, tells the rest of the story.

> . . . he resolutely refused medical attention and ignored his own painful injuries as he skillfully directed the action of the Marines. Realizing that radio communication was imperative, Second Lieutenant North fearlessly moved across the fire-swept terrain, climbed aboard the tank, and remained oblivious to the North Vietnamese rounds impacting around him as he retrieved the radio from atop the tank. . . .

After North made contact with support aircraft, he scooped up an M-79 grenade launcher and blasted away while shouting directions to his men. So effective was the counterattack, as the citation says, "that seven enemy soldiers were killed and the hostile fire silenced." North's ambushed platoon, meanwhile, suffered no deaths.

"North believed that the best way to avoid casualties was to return heavier fire than you were receiving, then rush into it so fast that you're exposed to enemy fire the minimum amount of time," recalls Ernie Tuten, a lance corporal machine gunner in North's platoon. "He practiced it. And it worked."

It worked on May 25, 1969, when the platoon just ahead of North's was ambushed in a cascade of enemy fire. They were hit by two 30-caliber machine guns, small arms, rocket-propelled grenades, directional mines and mortars from some one hundred NVAs on top of Hill 400. The platoon commander and a squad leader were immediately cut down; most of the forty other men went with them. The radios in the platoons behind were crackling, "Hit bad! Hit bad! Hit bad!"

"Kilo Two, Actual. This is Blue," North said, grabbing the handset from his radioman, using his radio code name, one that stuck with him throughout Vietnam. "Captain, the Second Platoon will move up."

There was never any doubt that North's Second Platoon—nicknamed "Blue's Bastards"—would move up.

"He insisted on immediate obedience," recalls Herrod. "A lot of officers would say, 'Go take that hill' or 'Go get that guy out of the bunker.' But North didn't do that. He didn't ask you to do anything he wasn't willing to do. When he said, 'Take that hill,' he was usually the first one there."

Following North and his order, the men in the Second Platoon dropped their packs and food. Grabbing just their weapons and ammunition, they started up the hill at a sprint clip. As they arrived at the point where the first platoon had been hit, they spread out and kept moving forward.

North had taught them that it was vital to keep in a straight line. Otherwise they would be shooting at each other. It was also the best way to keep track of his men. When calling in artillery support, he wouldn't make any mistakes and bring in fire on his own people.

"North was in the middle, with his .45 pistol in one hand, leading us," remembers Ernie Tuten. "He was telling us what to do, where to go, how to move. I was on the left with a machine gun; another machine gunner was on his right. There were about thirty-five of us and we just charged up the hill, throwing grenades, screaming."

It was a North standard operation: Don't waste time; don't hold a fixed position; don't dig in. Run right at them, shooting.

"North was the man to follow when the shit hit the fan," says Tuten.

The Second Platoon "screamers" stunned the North Vietnamese, who rapidly retreated to another ridge, giving North's men time to evacuate the wounded in the First Platoon. It also gave North time to regroup his forces and charge the new enemy position. The NVAs re-

treated again, this time onto a ridge entrenchment that had been prepared in advance.

Ollie North's Silver Star citation says the rest:

... Again reorganizing his men, Second Lieutenant North, with complete disregard for his
own safety, assumed the foremost assault position and, seemingly oblivious to the intense
machine gun fire impacting around him, led
his men against the hostile position.

But this time the enemy held its position tena-
ciously, throwing a heavy barrage of firepower
at North's beleagured troops. The Americans,
who meanwhile had been firing continuously
for fifteen minutes, were now running out of
ammunition. Unwilling to unnecessarily risk the
lives of his men, North halted the attack.

While the North Vietnamese continued to
rain small arms fire and RPGs, North directed
the resupply of his platoon and the evacuation
of wounded Marines. Phantom jets were soon
swooping low over the ridge, coming so close to
their targets that they cut trees in half all
around the Second Platoon. Then, says the official account:

North dauntlessly initiated a fourth assault by
his wearied men. Calmly braving the intense

fire of the tenacious hostile soldiers, he moved from one Marine to another, directing their fire and exhorting them to a last bold effort which, by his valorous perseverance, enabled his men to push the remainder of the North Vietnamese Army force from the ridgeline and to seize the objective.

Battles like this made North a young legend. "I'd follow Ollie North into hell," said one Marine, "because he's the only man I know who'd stand a chance of getting back."

Despite his strong, personal command on the battlefield, North was not one to get deeply involved with his men. If he asked someone how he was doing, "it was more like checking the oil," as one Marine remembers. "He wasn't the guy you went to talk about problems with your wife back home."

But it was Ollie's belief that when the battle began, your wife wouldn't matter. Only staying alive would. And at that, he had become a respected expert. "If my son had to go to war as a grunt—and I hope he never does—I'd want him to go with Ollie North," says Mark Traenor, a fellow Vietnam Marine veteran.

North was only twenty-six, but to his men, many of whom were only eighteen or nineteen, he was a senior figurehead. They relied on his fearless confidence, coming to believe that hitching up to North was the best way of getting out of the seemingly endless war alive. Though it was usual for men who had only two or three weeks left to their Vietnam tour to be allowed to stay behind on dangerous details, many of North's men preferred to go on a mission.

"Guys felt safer with Ollie North at the front than they did with anybody else at the rear," says Herrod. "I never saw him get nervous or make a mistake in the field. I'd follow him anywhere."

. . .

This wasn't what Randy Herrod thought when he first met Ollie North. Herrod was one of the many who were leery of this authoritarian, no-nonsense second lieutenant. "Here's this guy with chin straps on his helmet when no one wore them," Herrod recalls. "But he made *us* wear them. Everything was by the book. He insisted on instant obedience."

It wasn't just helmet straps. North was button-down all the way, an oddly old-fashioned leader in a war known for its free-wheeling, near-anarchic ways of battle. North's men weren't allowed to carry their ammunition as bandoliers around their chests. They couldn't remove the padding from their heavy flak jackets to make them lighter. They had to carry their grenades in pockets inside their jacket, not on their belts. They had to have a packet of battle dressing attached to the side of their helmets.

"And what really sticks in my head," says Herrod, "is that he shaved in the field—every day. Nobody else did."

But what Herrod and the others soon figured out was their boss was "meticulous about keeping us alive," as Herrod says. "All of his rules had that as their goal."

They learned it by experiencing the sinking sensation of being under heavy fire with a flaccid flak jacket or with ammunition that didn't fire because it had been dragged through the mud. Or seeing a grenade burst because a tree branch had snatched it off their belts. They learned by getting wounded and watching their helmet, with its life-saving bandages attached, roll down the hill. North ran a tight ship. But it worked.

"North is the reason a lot of us came back alive," says Herrod matter of factly. "He'd make sure the claymore mines and trip wires were laid out before he went to sleep and he checked them himself."

Ernie Tuten learned Ollie's lesson more rapidly than most.

"It was my first day in the field and I was coming in in a C-47 Seahorse helicopter. And boy was I loaded down. Three or four bandoliers of M-16 rounds, my rifle, six grenades, ten canteens full of water, ten c-rations, flak jacket and I don't know what else. I must have weighed five hundred pounds.

"Since this was last man on, first man off, I was supposed to be first off. And I did just what they taught us in training. When the door opened, I growled and ran off. Well, the guy on the copter didn't tell us that we were still fifteen feet above the ground. The only thing that saved me was that the bomb crater I landed in had a foot of water. It broke my fall, but I was stuck. With all the stuff I was carrying I didn't think I could move.

"And I remember looking up and seeing this rough-looking leatherneck standing on the rim of the crater looking down at me. He didn't help or offer to help. He just looked down and growled: 'Hurry up! Get out of there!' It was Lieutenant North."

As many people in Vietnam learned, North's voice had the ring of authority. And Tuten, the young recruit from Brunswick, Georgia, moved at its sound.

"If I hadn't moved when he told me, I'd have been a goner," Tuten remembers. "Because about the time that I'm getting out of the crater the raindrops starting falling—mortar rounds. One landed right in the crater where I thought I was stuck."

North developed a reputation for "knowing what was going to happen before it happened," as Randy Herrod puts it. But there was nothing magical about North's knowledge. He was a competent soldier with a good mind, a stern disciplinarian like his father, and a man focused on—some said possessed by—his mission. In North's magnifying glass gaze, there were only two objectives: defeat the enemy and keep his men alive.

Fellow Marine platoon leader Donald Moore would frequently hear North on the radio at night, signaling his movement through the bush. "He and Company Commander P.B. Goodwin had the coolest voices I've heard on the radio. Even under intense fire, North was calm," says Moore. "The only way I got a hint that he was nervous was when he was always going to one of his listening posts. He'd check and doublecheck his line. He'd set up two listening posts and then always go back and make sure there weren't any blind spots. And those men up there appreciated his company because it was the kind of job where you had to be ready to die. The whole idea was that you would get off a few rounds to warn the others before you got it."

North worked so continually at his job that he would sometimes go for days without true sleep. Or he would spend nights in which sleep was measured in minutes instead of hours.

"He lived with a mental checklist," says Moore. "He was machinelike in that. And if there were still things on his list, he wouldn't sleep. If somebody had to check the line late at night, it was always North. It would get to the point where some of the other lieutenants would simply say, 'Take a break, Ollie.'"

. . .

Donald Moore had been a philosophy major at George Mason University when the draft rules changed and he was unceremoniously bounced from metaphysics to the Marines. But he had had an uncle in the Marines and was predisposed to accepting the call like a good stoic.

In May of 1969, the bespectacled Moore touched down at a Marine base in Quangtri. He was a second lieutenant, Kilo Company, Third Battalion, Third Marines, and a philosopher-soldier.

Moore carried his gear into the transient officers' tent his first night, taking in everything. The tent—called a "hooch"—was a green canvas affair with wooden flooring. It normally slept six to eight men, but as Moore dropped his pack, only one Marine was there to greet him.

"I'm Ollie North." A lean, gritty apparition in muddy battle fatigues leaned toward Moore, thrusting a heavily bandaged hand out to shake. He smiled through the open spaces in his front teeth, explaining that he'd taken some shrapnel in his hand while attacking a bunker.

The introductions made, Moore began asking questions about Vietnam. North had answers, none of them reassuring.

"He frankly scared the hell out of me," remembers Moore.

Sitting alone in the quiet of candlelight, North enlightened Moore about the differences between what they had taught him at Basic School at Quantico and what was actually happening on the battlefront here in Vietnam.

"When you're under attack and call for artillery strikes," North said, "it won't come quickly like they told you. You can wait up to an hour for help."

Moore could feel his sense of dread building.

"And around here, there's no rice paddies and triple canopy jungle to hide in like they told you," North continued. "The fighting is in elephant grass and from rock outcroppings. Ridge to ridge."

Moore would soon learn first-hand why the men in his company were known as "ridge runners." He would learn what Mutters Ridge was, the hard way. And that the so-called jungle terrain of Vietnam he would come to know was in fact dry scrub, rock and hills. "Something like fighting in San Diego," Moore now explains.

The more North talked, the more Moore understood his responsibility. "It was extremely sobering," he recalls.

But when North told Moore that he should roust up some tabasco sauce and onions, the new lieutenant thought it was a big joke. "You'll have a fair number of Hispanics in your outfit," North explained. "They like their rations spiced up a bit. And you'll make a good first impression if you get off the chopper with it."

North had all the angles of modern war covered, Moore decided.

"They probably taught you a lot about arms and tanks and all the artillery backup you'll get," Ollie concluded, like a coach preparing a quarterback. "But sometimes a battle can be decided by a lieutenant who gets up and says to his men, 'Let's go, boys!' "

After their hour-long discussion, the two men walked toward the nearby "officers' club" for a drink. An officer's ration card allowed three bottle of free booze per month, not an easy quota to fill when you're on the front, North explained. They walked between rows of tightly packed tents on a walkway constructed from discarded artillery shell boxes. It was warm and the night was clear. They could hear muffled voices from the officers' club hooch.

"Watch this," North said, motioning for Moore to stop and listen. The veteran lieutenant bent and picked up a rock. Moore followed his gaze to the corrugated tin roof of the hooch. Then, with a practiced stroke, North lobbed a rock onto the roof.

"It made this clunkety-clunk, clunkety-clunk sound as it rolled down," recalls Moore.

The two men walked into a hooch frozen in silence. All the Marines were on the floor, arms over their head. North broke out laughing.

"There was a lot of talk around about fragging," explains Moore. "And these guys thought that a grenade had just been tossed onto their tent and they were being fragged."

North, always an unusual cross of stern Scottish taskmaster and Irish pixie, had been letting off some of the steam of combat.

. . .

By the time North arrived in Vietnam in December 1968, the land between the 17th and 18th parallels had been established as a Demilitarized Zone, the first step toward so-called peace.

But the area was still a hot spot of conflict. One night the DMZ became a "Hot Tamale," the code name of a secret operation to be headed by Lieutenant North.

"Tonight, we've got to take us a North Vietnamese prisoner," he told his men.

The word had come from Washington that the United States needed proof that the North Vietnamese were operating in the DMZ in violation of the tentative agreement being hammered out in Paris by Henry Kissinger and Le Duc Tho. Every leatherneck in the area knew the NVA regulars were still in the zone, but they needed proof.

Ollie North, as usual, was the first to enter the minds of the brass choosing the detail. His platoon was usually the lead platoon when the company did "road sweeps" in bloody "Leatherneck Square." And it had been chosen as the honor platoon for the changing of command at Northern I Corps near Hue. Now it was given the dubious honor of conducting Operation Hot Tamale.

North asked for, and received, fifteen volunteers from his platoon. They rode northward in a truck, bouncing over the moonscaped land until they arrived at the 18th parallel. The men's faces were smeared black and they had donned camouflage fatigues for the night mission. When the truck suddenly stopped they slipped out into the dark on foot. For hours, the "Killer Squad" wandered silently through the bush of the DMZ's no-man's land, but it found no enemy. The NVA was obviously skillfully hiding its presence from expected American search parties.

It was North's idea to move into North Vietnam itself. He dispatched everyone back to base and took only one volunteer with him. North and the other Marine easily penetrated enemy lines. They quietly approached an NVA camp and grabbed a soldier on guard duty, rushing him back with them to base. "He got the job done," says a Marine who was part of the secret operation.

That was what characterized Oliver North— his ability to get the job done without examining it. "Blue" North was by no means blind to the higher meaning of his actions. But in Vietnam he simply didn't have time, nor did he think it was his job as a lieutenant to ponder them.

When astronaut Neil Armstrong set foot on the moon on July 20, 1969, student philosopher

Don Moore commented to North. "It's strange that we're advanced enough to be walking in outer space but we're still fighting primitive jungle wars."

North, not yet the eloquent geopolitical spokesman he was to become, merely grunted: "Weird."

Father Laboon confirms that young North restricted himself to fighting a difficult war. "Some of the senior officers would sometimes say to me," recalls Laboon, "that we tell our soldiers that they came over here to fight Communism and now we are turning the nation back over to a pseudo-Communistic country. What can we tell them? But I never heard North talk like that. He wouldn't allow himself to get into that kind of conversation—probably for fear it was bad for morale. He'd just say: 'We're Marines. We were sent over here to do a job. And that's all there is to it.'"

That job was, of course, getting harder and harder to perform. Oliver North and hundreds of thousands of others were risking their lives for a war the American government had already decided was politically untenable, even unwinnable. North always believed the United States and its ally, South Vietnam, were winning the war on the battlefield, but he spent little time worrying about it. He maintained an abiding faith in his superiors. He followed orders and won battle after battle as his country lost the war, in Washington and Paris.

By the time Ollie left Vietnam in November 1969 after a year of combat, he received a plaque from the men he was leaving behind:

To the Big Blue Bastard
from All the Little Blue Bastards

Ollie returned to the States a skillful, hardened combat veteran. But there were no parades to march in like those that greeted his father after World War II. Awarded some of the nation's highest honors and wounded at least twice, North was assigned the job of teaching young Marines what he had learned in Vietnam.

He was dispatched to Quantico, Virginia, to the Marine Officer Basic School where he himself had been trained. He taught what he had learned in combat: the most important task of an officer in war is to keep his men alive so that they can continue to fight.

One trait that came naturally to North, but which was heightened by his Annapolis training and the crucible of Vietnam, was loyalty to his comrades.

The quality was so strong that North announced to his superiors that he was flying back to Vietnam. He had volunteered to be a character witness for a young soldier accused of sixteen counts of murder allegedly perpetrated against Vietnamese civilians during combat.

Randy Herrod was the one in trouble. On February 19, 1970, the day before he was to receive the Silver Star for saving North's life, Herrod was arrested and thrown in the brig. It seems that after North had left Vietnam, Herrod had been transferred to another unit operating in the south of the country. There it was a different war with a new enemy. Instead of fighting North Vietnamese Regulars who wore uniforms, he was fighting often invisible guerrillas and irregulars, none advertising their hostility. Women and children in a village frequently threw grenades as the Marines approached.

When Herrod and three other American Marines entered the village of Son Thang, thirty miles south of Danang, the enemy was all around. The fighting began and ended fiercely. Sixteen women and children died in the firefight.

It had been only three months since *The New York Times* revealed on November 16, 1969, the massacre of three hundred women and children in a small Vietnamese village called My Lai. The opprobrium for the act was universal.

The day before, 250,000 antiwar demonstrators had marched on Washington.

After Randy Herrod was put in jail, observers began calling the Son Thang affair "the Marines' My Lai." Some Marine Corps brass, embarrassed at the publicity, wanted this incident behind them. A rapid conviction would ease the public pressure.

"They wanted the death penalty for Randy," says Denzel Garrison, the Oklahoma attorney who signed on to defend the young Marine. "We were able to get hold of documents which suggested that the brass wanted the thing over with quickly."

The prosecuting attorney was able to do that with the other three defendants in the case, all of whom were swiftly convicted of murder. "The prosecutor was an Ivy League type who got a bronze star for his work on the case—though they kept that quiet," says Garrison, who had also become involved in the Herrod case through loyalty. He had fought in Korea and when wounded, was carried through a minefield to safety by Randy Herrod's uncle.

Oliver North had a similar debt to repay. Without concern for the attitude of the Marine brass, North paid his own way from Quantico to San Francisco, then hitched a ride on a military transport to Danang, where the trial was scheduled to begin in August. A reporter, learning why North had come, asked the young second lieutenant if he had ever read *Catch 22*, the black comedy about military absurdity in World War II.

North smiled. "One of my favorite books."

Ollie immediately volunteered to help the defense in any way he could. But while awaiting orders from Garrison and co-counsel Gene Stipe, he decided there was no reason to waste good combat time in Vietnam. North volunteered to do some free-lance patrolling with a Marine helicopter unit.

"They were dangerous missions," recalls Garrison. "I was a little worried we'd lose our star witness."

The copter unit North worked with had as its insignia a skull and crossbones, with the words "Swift Silent Death." "We brought that up at Herrod's trial," Garrison says. "Here we train these guys to protect themselves and kill—Swift Silent Death—and then we second-guess them all the time afterwards."

North survived his patrols and provided Herrod's defense with valuable aid. He sent out a poll to the officers on base, asking what were Herrod's chances of receiving a fair trial. The response was 29 to 1 saying he wouldn't get one. It was North who revealed to the defense the fact that the U.S. military had a hamlet classification system. If a Vietnamese village was all friendly, it was designated a *I*. If mostly friendly, it was *II*. Mostly unfriendly, *III*. If it was an *enemy* village, a *IV*.

Son Thang, North discovered, was classified *IV*. It was enemy Vietcong territory despite the fact that it was in South Vietnam. "It meant a Marine entering a *I* village with all sympathizers would have a slightly different outlook on life than one entering a *IV* with all enemies," Garrison explains.

Garrison and Stipe were able to mount an impressive defense for the young corporal. And by putting North on the stand, they were able to tell the court the story of how Herrod had won his Silver Star. "Ollie gave Herrod credit for saving his life," says Stipe. "I think the court was impressed."

North sat in the stand, his back upright, his hands on his knees, for thirty minutes at a stretch. It was over a hundred degrees. His uniform was spotless, his tie plumbed straight. He didn't even sweat.

"You have to understand what Lieutenant North was doing," Herrod says today. "I mean, there were all these secret communications from the Pentagon to the commanding general in Danang telling him to convict me. . . . The prosecutor got a Bronze Star for convicting the other guys. So anybody who says that Ollie North is superambitious just doesn't know him. He cared more for his men than his commission. He would have done the same for any of the men who served under him."

The trial lasted eleven days and North was there for all of it.

Herrod was acquitted—and North retained his faith in the Marines and their frustrating mission in Southeast Asia, one that would shape his mind and his extraordinary career from then on.

*Five*

---

# The Fast Track

IN THE FALL OF 1969, OLIVER NORTH RE-
turned home from his one-year tour in Vietnam
with the Silver and Bronze Stars and two Purple
Hearts on his chest and several pieces of shrapnel in his back.

He was only twenty-six, the father of a toddler
daughter named Tait and a "rising star" in the
Marine Corps, as one colleague recalls it. He
had learned a considerable amount in that year
in Southeast Asia, including the old military
truism that a good war is the best path to the
top. He had made his first lieutenant grade, had
shown valor in combat and given evidence of
his patriotism and character, qualities the Corps

admired. North had just been named an instructor at the prestigious Basic School at Quantico, Virginia, his own alma mater and the incubator for the Corps' elite officer ranks.

Ollie North was on the fast track.

For someone who let himself dream that someday he could become the Commandant of Marines, he was headed in exactly the right direction.

At the sprawling Virginia training base, Ollie immediately developed a reputation for hard, almost obsessive, work. Fellow instructors, who were battle-trained veterans like himself, liked Ollie despite his laserlike approach. And the fresh young lieutenants headed for the still-savage Vietnam war appreciated his knowledge, which could spell the difference between life and death.

"He knew the material cold," remembers Mark Treanor, a fellow instructor at Quantico, now an attorney in Virginia.

North drilled the future warriors tirelessly but never asked them to do anything he wouldn't. Patrolling was a key to staying alive in combat, North believed, and he led his students regularly through the make-believe jungles of Virginia with the energy of a young recruit. Small unit actions, night ambushes and clandes-

tine combat—the ABCs of Vietnam—were his
favorites.

"He absolutely loved teaching tactics," says a
former Quantico student. "He was into it eighteen hours a day."

All two hundred instructors on the Quantico
base were gung-ho Marines, otherwise they
wouldn't have had the assignment. But with his
natural enthusiasm, North stood out among
even such professional competition. "You noticed him right away," remembers Bob Pfeiffer,
a fellow instructor and now Lacrosse coach at a
New England college. Pfeiffer and Ollie often
played basketball during the lunch hour. Just as
he had in boxing, Ollie played with "no finesse,"
says Pfeiffer, "but he was a real scrambler."

The dramatic tendency in North, the talent
for highlighting his activities, was obvious even
then. To simulate the madness of the war, North
invented antic methods of teaching that held
his students' rapt attention. He would sometimes charge through a classroom door, canoe
paddle in hand and pants legs rolled up. "Better
roll up your pants!" he shouted. "It's too late for
your shoes! This guy's really slinging it today."

Other times, he would jump up on his desk,
M-16 in hand, and begin rapid firing into the
crowd of students. Only after the green young
lieutenants pulled their heaving chests off the

ground did he tell them the bullets were blanks. Other times, he maneuvered a big Harley-Davidson motorcycle—his favorite Quantico transport—right into the classroom. Occasionally, he would lean back with the prerogatives of power while a base secretary brought him coffee.

"He was a showman and the lieutenants ate it up," says Treanor, who had been a North classmate at Annapolis. "But he did it because Vietnam was a deadly business and he wanted to teach them to stay alive."

Treanor recalls times when he and North would return to their offices after twelve or fifteen grueling hours in the field. "We would be completely exhausted, our faces black with paint and our camouflage gear still on," he says. Instead of going home and cracking open a cool one, the Marines rehashed the day, selecting out what they did right and what went wrong. "When you're entrusted with the lives of men— I now know they're just kids—it makes you work night and day. It's an enormous responsibility."

Work, usually excessive, always enervating, was and still is the hallmark of Ollie North. "The instructors at the Basic School are probably the top of the heap as far as the Marine Corps goes," says one veteran Marine who knew North. "So you've got forty captains who are all very competitive, tough and bright. And Ollie got ahead of them all by work. I mean he practically lived there. He slept in his office. He didn't go home except maybe on weekends. If you're willing to do that, I suppose you can outperform others. But how many people are willing to? Just Ollie."

North displayed the same enthusiasm for play—even outlandish play—in the few moments he allotted to it. At one graduation party for students, he found himself in line playing the Navy game of "Carrier Quals," shorthand for the qualification test of landing a fast Navy jet on a moving carrier.

When it was his turn, North ran at the cleared table like a long jumper, his arms extended like the wings of the plane he was mimicking. Just before hitting the "deck," he leapt forward, head first. North landed with such ferocity that he shot the length of the table before sailing into the wild blue yonder—hitting a nearby wall. To the cheers of onlookers, North was soon up, his face bloodied. He smiled to all and flew in for another hard-hitting landing.

"We played tough games," says Treanor, "but we weren't one dimensional. These people were all young, tough, energetic guys. You work very hard at Basic School and afterwards you let your hair down. It was a little like cowboys coming in to town after months on the range."

Friday night boxer. Combat hero. Symbolic cowboy. In a branch of the service that was itself intensely competitive, North was the archetypical competitor.

The desire to win was implicit in everything North did. But some felt it was part of his powerful personal ambition, that he was always propelling himself forward for promotion. Rob Pfeiffer—who unlike North did not choose the Marines as a lifelong career—interprets some of North's moves as a desire to "make rank," as the Corps calls it.

Recalling their lunchtime basketball games in which the base commanding officer often participated, Pfeiffer says: "I fed the ball to the CO because I couldn't shoot. Ollie passed it to him because he wanted to make rank."

There is still considerable controversy over whether "making rank" was the prime motivator in North's case. Especially his rewarding habit of finding a senior "Godfather" at each of his posts. But less cynical friends of Ollie, in and out of the Marines, remind everyone that loyalty is much more important to him—even at the risk of damage to his career.

Attorney Denzil Garrison emphasizes that when North flew from Quantico to Danang in the summer of 1970 at his own expense to testify on behalf of his former gunnery corporal

Randy Herrod, he was flying in the face of official Corps policy.

"He had nothing to gain from the Corps for his testimony," says Garrison. "And much to lose."

. . .

*Semper Fi,* always loyal, is a Marine Corps motto that Oliver North took very seriously. It was particularly tested during the Vietnam War, when North was a combat leatherneck during the most vehemently antimilitary period in American history.

Vietnam may have been a good war for making Marine rank, but it wasn't one for making friends in the rest of the community. Worn by dissension, disillusioned that the war wasn't being won—in the conventional World War I and II molds—the nation gave little respect to the men fighting it. It was, in the common parlance, a "dirty war," one to which civilian lives were often sacrificed for military reasons.

News about the My Lai massacre broke just two weeks before Ollie's posting to Quantico. And just sixty miles away, a quarter of a million Americans marched around the White House to protest against everything Ollie North stood for.

THE DEFIANT PATRIOT

In May 1970, four student dissenters at Kent State University were killed by edgy National Guardsmen. In 1971, a military court found Lieutenant William L. Calley guilty of murdering twenty-two Vietnamese civilians at My Lai. *The New York Times* printed the once-secret Pentagon Papers only months after that. The war against Communism in Southeast Asia was contentious, divisive, frustrating and incomprehensible to most.

But not to Ollie North. "He always argued that the Corps was the bastion of American freedom and patriotism," recalls Rob Pfeiffer.

As the My Lai conviction cast dishonor on the American uniform, North decided it was time to fight back. This time the battle was against a domestic enemy that was sullying the name of all servicemen, including the Marines. That new enemy, North was convinced, was the American media.

Ollie and two other young Quantico officers, all Vietnam vets, drafted and mailed off long letters of protest to the three television networks, accusing them of broadcasting news reports on Vietnam that were unfair to American servicemen. The media, the angry Marines wrote, has paraded before the public "confessions and accusations from those who feel an overwhelming guilt about their participation and involvement in Southeast Asia."

North and his buddies insisted that despite the difficulties involved, American combat troops fought with decency. "Each of us has had ample opportunity to both lead and observe Americans in combat," they said. "Yet none of us have ever witnessed, participated in, or been cognizant of a single instance wherein any Vietnamese noncombatant, North or South, was treated in anything less than a human fashion. We believe that the American public should know this."

The three Marine officers asked for equal time to tell their side of the story on national television. But they were rebuffed.

Only one media power, the conservative columnist and editor of the *National Review,* William F. Buckley, Jr., responded, offering North and his buddies a chance to appear on his television show, *Firing Line.* "It's the only time I've ever seen Buckley keep quiet," recalls Pfeiffer. "It became the Ollie North Show. But he did a good job of stating our position."

Captain North was in his summer-dress khaki Marine uniform, with cross-chest Sam Brown belt, looking tan and athletic. With his hands clasped loosely on his lap, his legs splayed and shoulders hunched, he looked uncomfortable.

But under the lights, the intensity in his eyes shone.

North's syntax may not have been as elegant as that of his fellow officers, one a graduate of Exeter and Princeton, the other of Andover and Brown. But the young captain displayed his knowledge and sincerity, insisting that the American serviceman was being abused by the American press—to the detriment of national interest.

"I never witnessed a single ear being cut off, a single round being shot against a man without a rifle," North told the national television audience. In fact, he reminded everyone of the Marines' helping role, that sometimes "we went into villages for no other reason" than to deliver medical supplies.

He pointed out that even though all Vietnamese civilians had supposedly been removed from a "so-called free-fire zone," and that everyone left was supposed to be the enemy, he and his men continued their policy of only firing at "known armed enemy."

"I watched him on television and I was impressed," says a fellow Annapolis grad, now at Marine Corps headquarters in Washington. "I was proud that he did it."

•  •  •

## The Fast Track

The last American troops left Vietnam in the summer of 1972, the single fact that changed the face of American politics and the lives of most Marines.

The following year the military draft was discontinued, and in November of 1973 Congress tried to hobble the foreign-policy power of the White House by passing the War Powers Act.

People were turning their minds back to more mundane pursuits—except for Ollie North, who continued on his fast track as if the war were still on. He had already made captain. He had been a company commander at Quantico, attended Amphibious Warfare School and had taken a Nuclear and Chemical Weapons Employment course. Now thirty, he had the option of seeking a Marine desk job. Instead, North chose a tour of hardship duty almost as rough as any war.

The place was the Japanese island of Okinawa, where 103,000 Japanese had been killed holding out against American Marines and the Army in World War II, until the remaining 20,000 either committed hara-kiri or surrendered in the last strategic battle of the Pacific War.

Now, in January 1974, part of the island had been converted to a jungle warfare training area, and Ollie North was chosen to head it. His

official assignment was Camp Commander and
Officer-in-Charge, Third Marine Division
Schools Detachment, Northern Training Area.
The Marines were fearful that peacetime duty
could soften their men, and they had given
Ollie North the assignment to hone the men's
skills by creating a warlike atmosphere.

The Northern Training Area was located in
the rough mountain ridges and jungles of the
seventy-by-fifteen mile island. On its northern-
most, rugged portion, the Marines had established a training ground in counterinsurgency
and small unit tactics for the elite fighting forces
of all the American military—the Marines, the
Green Berets, the Navy Seals. Captain North
had to leave his family behind for this unusual
post in the Pacific wilds.

"It was the toughest thing I've ever done in
my life," says an instructor who worked there
under North, and now a Marine major. "It was
a real frontier experience."

The camp was unofficially known as "the end-
of-the-world."

"The only thing they had were a few quonset
huts," recalls Lt. Colonel Ken Estes, a Marine
then stationed at the nearest permanent
Okinawa base, Camp Schwab, fifteen miles to
the south. "These guys lived up there for
months at a time. There was no civilization."

## The Fast Track

Every month a group of a thousand men, a full batallion, would rotate through the camp. With his eighty instructors and support personnel, North would run them through a grueling eighteen-hour-a-day, seven-day-a-week package of courses ranging from survival training to rough terrain navigation, ambushing and rapelling down cliffs and walls. The men learned to climb mountains, build rope bridges across rivers, travel rapidly and silently over unfriendly terrain.

One exercise called the "amphibious raid package," was the toughest, lasting eighteen continuous days. "It was eighteen days of nonstop surgical strike practice—how to raid, rescue and evacuate an enemy target a la Entebbe," says a former Okinawa instructor. "We'd practice it over and over again. You hardly got any sleep.'

"It is essentially a month-long obstacle course," a Marine Corps spokesman says of the school. And Captain Oliver North was known as its "top gun."

"He was very, very good," says a Marine major who worked under North. "He could—and did—everything the instructors did. That meant *everything,* from a hundred mile march to rapelling down a hundred-and-sixty foot mountain side."

Again, North brought not only dedication to the work, but his Philmont pranksterism—the innate show business "shticks" that released the tension. It was the same antic edge he had honed at Quantico. When demonstrating rapelling to the young Marines, for example, he came down the mountain firing his rifle, or dropped out of a helicopter doing the same.

Since the training was basically anti-guerrilla —and North was confident that Vietnam wouldn't be the last place American Marines would fight Communist guerrillas—he made sure his students understood the philosophy of Marxist insurgency. He introduced them to the psychology of the enemy, then made everyone read the writings of Mao Tse-tung and the late Cuban leftist Che Guevera. In fact, North's favorite ambush technique was one Guevera called "The Minuet," a mobile ambush in which attackers circled their prey and fired from four or five different places at once.

As North spoke to the students, a camouflaged Marine suddenly charged out from behind a curtain, firing his rifle in all directions.

"That's an ambush," North explained to the surprised trainees. "It's swift, violent and destructive." The one place not to be, he explained, was "the killing zone," the area of the ambush where there is nothing but flying lead.

## The Fast Track

To outsiders, even to war-hardened Marines, the NTA camp run by North was a thing apart, a kind of self-made psychological inferno. "They lived like animals up there," says Lieutenant Colonel Estes. "If the top brass were going to visit, you had to give them plenty of notice so they could clean up their act. And when we brought up supplies, I wouldn't let my guys stay there for more than a week. It wasn't just North. *All* the NTA guys were crazy."

The troops, who rotated in and out for a month, had only to survive the camp's intensity for thirty days. But instructors, including North, were forced to tolerate the camp's relentless pace for as much as a year. "He didn't take breaks, he didn't eat, he didn't sleep," says a former survival teacher. "Ollie worked himself to a frazzle. I watched as he went from something like a hundred-and-seventy pounds to one-thirty."

It was on Okinawa that Ollie North suffered the "breakdown" which has been the subject of continuing speculation. The unrelieved strain of the NTA was obviously excessive, but according to some, it actually caused an emotional trauma. One story has North stumbling naked through the jungle outpost, a .45 pistol in hand, mumbling something about wanting to kill himself.

"There was no doubt that he was in bad physical shape by the time he left," says an instructor who worked under North and who insists his identity be protected. "But that other story is bullshit. I lived with the guy. If it had happened I would have known about it. He was never on emergency leave. He was never relieved of his duties. Sure, he was physically sick, but I saw him the days he got on the airplane at Kadena Air Force Base and he was pretty damn lucid."

Another Marine friend explains away the persistent rumors this way: "He just pushes himself so hard. He's the epitome of the can-do Marine. But his can-do can lead to his *undoing.* He literally ran himself into the ground in Okinawa."

Whatever the cause, a weak, emaciated North boarded a plane in Okinawa in December 1974 headed for the States. Not long after, he was a patient at Bethesda Naval Hospital in the Maryland suburbs of Washington. He stayed for a period of three weeks of "voluntary hospitalization"—from December 16 to January 7, 1975—and was discharged, according to the Marine Corps, as "fit for full duty."

The Marine Corps has refused to share North's medical records with anyone, explaining that a Marine officer's hospitalization record is kept separate from his official personnel "jacket." North's records they state are in the hands of the Medical Officer of the Marine Corps. "In view of the Privacy Act, any further questions concerning medical treatment must be referred to Lieutenant Colonel North."

. . .

For the next three-and-a-half years, Oliver North did something he hadn't done since his Annapolis days. He sat behind a desk. Assigned to Marine headquarters in the shadow of the Pentagon, he spent most of that time in a dingy fourth floor office in Arlington, Virginia, which he shared with a half dozen other Marines.

"Pigeons roosted in the rafters above," recalls David Evans, who worked just down the hall and is now a military affairs writer for the *Chicago Tribune*. "People around the place used to talk about having pigeon shit in their in-boxes."

Only three blocks from the Pentagon, the Marine Corps HQ is a poor stepsister to that massive stone structure. But the meager facilities were symbolic of the Corps' action orientation. For North, who knew the byways of his service, it was obvious he hadn't been shunted aside. His assignment—the Manpower Plans and Policy Directorate—was part of his fast track to the top.

With the draft cancelled, North was charged

with evaluating Marine manpower needs and figuring out how to fill them. "The manpower people were trying to stop the hemorrhaging. And North was again at the center of the action," Evans relates. "Ollie was a very energetic guy. Fourteen to eighteen hours a day, six days a week."

Evans became fascinated with North and his intriguing personality. "Ollie was more intensely focused than most people," he says. "He was like the magnifying glass you played with in the sun as a kid. He was always in focus. Always there. He prided himself on being the indispensable man."

Apparently North was almost indispensable. His manpower work at that crucial point in the nation's antimilitary sentiment won him another Marine decoration, the Meritorious Service Medal. It was granted, said the award, not only for his "exhausting work schedule" and "perceptive analysis," but for briefings to his superiors, including the Marine Commandant himself.

Ollie was being noticed by the brass, a cause for jealousy among his co-workers. "He had the habit of wearing his ambition on his sleeve," says one critic who knew North during this mid-to-late 1970s period.

In July 1978, ten years after he left Annapolis,

North was promoted to major and posted to Camp Lejeune, North Carolina as Operations Officer of the Third Battalion, Eighth Marines.

It was no dead-end, or sideways, career move. Lejeune was the Marine's main amphibious warfare training center. "It was an important job," says former Lieutenant Colonel Evans. "Ollie was definitely in the mainstream. The move from headquarters to Lejeune was a sign of upward mobility, a strong robust career progression—probably in the top quarter of Marine officers."

North's spiraling career advancement stemmed from his work, but he had also developed the skill of gravitating toward power—to make sure that his efforts were appreciated by the right people. Ollie always had what the Marines call a "Godfather," someone of rank who would advance his cause.

At Quantico, it was Colonel Charles Schultze, a former battalion commander in Vietnam and North's CO at Basic School. At headquarters in Washington, Ollie had met several top Marines including the Commandant, General Robert Barrow, who once labeled North "Mr. Enthusiasm" because of his lively, upbeat briefings. Ollie apparently knew others as well.

"I hadn't seen Ollie until sometime in 1975," recalls Roger Charles, a fellow member of the

Annapolis boxing team. "A bunch of us were in Matt Kane's bar in Washington for a Marine birthday party when Ollie came in with a couple of heavy colonels. The general, as it turned out, was the assistant commandant of the Marine Corps."

At Camp Lejeune, Ollie's commanding officer, Lieutenant Colonel John S. Grinalds, now a brigadier general, was destined to become another fan of the intrepid Marine. As Operations Officer of the battalion, North had a wide range of duties, all of which he accomplished with his usual zeal, working day and night to lighten the burden of his CO. He quickly developed a reputation for reliability and even came to the attention of Major General Ed Bronars, then at Lejeune.

If anyone can be given the credit for moving Ollie North from the gritty Marine ranks and into the pristine inner circle of the White House it is General Bronars.

North had been at Marine headquarters from January 1975 through June 1978, and at Lejeune until July 1980. It was the next career move—to the Naval War College—that marked North's rise into the stratosphere of power. His commanding officer, John Grinalds, was obviously instrumental in that vital move.

"I wouldn't say that it means you will become

a general," says General Grinalds about the military graduate school, "but it is a normal part of the preparation for higher rank. It's a good sign that you're on your way up."

In the middle of the summer of 1980, Ollie North, now thirty-six, was back on an elite campus twelve years after he had graduated Annapolis barely in the middle of his class. Of 20,000 Marine officers, he was one of only 20 selected to attend the class of '80–'81 of this intellectual finishing school for promising military men. Almost ninety percent of those who enroll in the intensive ten-month course go on to become flag officers, even heads of their respective services. Ollie's dream of someday becoming America's top Marine was no longer a middie's fantasy.

Founded in 1884, the Naval War College stands on a promontory overlooking Narragansett Bay in Newport, Rhode Island. North had three major areas of study to choose from— Strategy and Policy; National Security Decisions; and Operations. Ollie, always the activist, chose Operations—getting Marines and sailors in the right place at the right time.

But it was not a formal course that would help catapult North into the national arena. It was more likely a touch of serendipity. Whether by foresight or accident, Ollie wrote a paper about the recommissioning of World War II battle-ships, an unusual subject for a mud-and-march Vietnam grunt. Strangely, this was also the pet project of the new Secretary of the Navy, John Lehman, who had just been appointed by in-coming President Reagan.

Lehman was a lot like North—active, aggressive, physical and young. The two reportedly met briefly before North's June 1981 graduation at a three-day symposium sponsored by the Secretary, in which three hundred distinguished guests mingled on the historic Rhode Island campus.

Shortly after, the Corps was asked to submit a few names of Marine officers, one of whom would be chosen to serve on the staff of the National Security Council.

"General Ed Bronars—who knew Ollie from Lejeune and liked him—was head of manpower assignment when the call for the National Security Council position came in," explains David Evans. "He would have been the one making the recommendation. And Marine Commandant Barrows would have taken Bronars' recommendation. The case was pretty well scrubbed by the time Barrows got it."

General Bronars remembers the selection. "Oliver North was an exceptional officer with an exceptional record," recalls General Bronars, now retired and head of the Navy Relief Society. "And I would be surprised if he weren't at the top of my list."

That, perhaps with the added recommendation of North's powerful peer, Secretary of the Navy John Lehman, made its way through NSC channels. All the passion Oliver North had expended on behalf of the Marines and his country for almost two decades, had now borne fruit—sweeter and more enticing than the young man from Philmont could ever have dreamed.

On August 4, 1981, at the age of thirty-seven, Major Oliver Laurence North reported for duty at the White House, beginning a tour of such magnitude that it would shake the nation.

*Six*

---

# The NSC:
# Days of Glory

OLLIE NORTH'S BEING NAMED TO THE NA-
tional Security Council was, in a way, a political
fluke.

As heady as his White House appointment
seemed, North had actually crossed the Poto-
mac from Marine headquarters in Arlington for
one particular assignment. He had been
brought to the White House on TDY, temporary duty, to help convince Congress to sell
America's most sophisticated electronic surveil-
lance plane—the AWAC—to Saudi Arabia.

"We never had such specific lobbying duties
here until the President asked us to lead the
AWAC fight on the Hill," explains Richard

Allen, former NSC staff chief and Ollie North's boss. "Since the NSC was always short of staff and funds, we often 'borrowed' people from other agencies whenever we had to act quickly. I had one of my military guys get three officers to come over and help on the AWAC thing. The Marines sent North. And they paid his salary."

In his first months, Ollie didn't take the NSC by storm nor did he singlehandedly sway the Congress to vote the President's way. His initial work at the White House was quite prosaic. "We needed the extra people and he was sent over to hold charts and carry the briefcases for our people going to the Hill," says Allen. "He was a military grunt, a junior officer whose job it was to assist the mechanical and logistical function of lobbying members of Congress."

By accident, North met Major General Richard V. Secord, later to play such a crucial role in North's career. Then a deputy assistant secretary of defense, Secord was the Pentagon's point man in the AWAC lobbying effort.

Some around North have always maintained that his greatest asset was a hovering guardian angel. A chance friendship with the son of the Naval Academy's soccer coach had taken him to Annapolis. A miracle had saved his life in a car crash that killed his friend. An eighteen-year-old kid had dragged him to safety in a firefight in Vietnam. And now, an academic paper on battleship recommissioning had caught the eye of the Secretary of the Navy and secured him an enviable White House berth.

"I know of at least two other officers who would have been much better choices for the NSC job," says David Evans, a retired lieutenant colonel who worked with North at Marine headquarters. "Ollie wasn't regarded as an in-depth thinker who was patient with nuances. He was action-oriented, the John Wayne type. And the NSC wasn't necessarily the best place for that kind of person. It was for the guy who can say, 'Hey, wait a minute, let's think this through.' We had other middle-grade officers in the Marine Corps who were more familiar with world politics, better writers, more prescient thinkers. Ollie was good, but not necessarily the best."

But forces at work within the Reagan Administration were enhancing the value of an "action" man like North. The National Security Council was changing rapidly. Once a select group of thinkers who gathered information then offered the President reasoned options, it had now assumed a new, more aggressive, face.

The new NSC was becoming the dagger-point of the Reagan Doctrine. The President had called for the end of passive acceptance of

Soviet expansionism. America would now take the initiative and roll back Communism wherever possible. But the mammoth Washington bureaucracies—the State Department, the Defense Department, even the CIA—were finding it difficult to adjust to the new initiative. Perhaps most important, all three were addicted to "leaks," as was the U.S. Congress.

Reagan wanted a small, effective, "think-action" tank that was physically and spiritually close to him. One that would operate effectively—and secretly. And unlike the CIA, one that was not constantly subject to congressional oversight. The NSC was the President's obvious choice, and with it, he inherited Ollie North.

"North was supposed to be gone by early 1982 because he wasn't part of the professional staff and wasn't intended as such," Allen, apparently no fan of North's, recalls.

But with North's charmed existence, quite the opposite took place. Allen left the NSC in December of 1981 and was replaced by Judge William Clark. The long-time Reagan associate was too busy learning the ropes to worry about a junior grade Marine major on temporary duty.

North stayed and made himself useful, gradually earning a reputation as a doer. He worked long hours, often arriving at his desk at 7:30 in the morning and not leaving until midnight.

Twelve hours was a "minimum" day; many were fourteen to sixteen hours.

"Ollie was extremely hardworking and dedicated," recalls fellow NSC staffer Roger Fontaine. "He did stuff that other people would turn up their noses at because it wasn't high-powered or impressive enough. He'd do whatever job had to be done and you certainly couldn't say that for the others."

As time progressed, so did the importance of the NSC to Ronald Reagan. "During the Reagan Administration," writes author James Bamford "the NSC's transformation from an advisory and coordinating body into an operational one, a kind of 'Mission: Impossible' force was completed."

Once again, Ollie had found himself in the right place at the right time. North was the outstanding "Mission: Impossible" type on the NSC staff. He handled one brown "action folder" from the President after another, to demonstrate his skills and personal charm.

"I always thought North was the right man for the job he had. He was very bright and he was an operational person—he could get the job done," explains Raymond Tanter, a colleague of North's at the NSC and now a professor of political science. "Some might argue that you don't need an operational man at the NSC, that North was miscast. But as we know, he wasn't miscast at all."

As he made his presence felt, his full personality—including a dry wit and youthful playfulness—began to make its mark.

"North had a swashbuckling air," says Linda Chavez, former White House public liaison officer. "Like somebody out of another era. A romantic character who would rescue damsels in distress."

North's braggadacio and theatricality surfaced regularly. When he called the Pentagon, he sometimes identified himself as "Dr. North from the White House." Annapolis classmate Lieutenant Colonel Ken Estes, recounts another tale. "Once he chewed out a three-star Air Force General," Estes recalled. "But the general found out that he had been had by a lowly major and he called Ollie back and gave it to him."

Ollie also had a penchant for an occasional tall tale, which he enjoyed telling the unsuspecting. An NSC colleague relates one of North's geopolitical fish stories.

"I remember one guy coming out of North's office with a worried look on his face," he says. "He was aghast that North had captured five Iranians in Europe and was holding them in a

Young Oliver "Larry" North on the occasion of his first communion in front of the Church of the Sacred Heart.
COURTESY: MRS. EVELYN RONSANI

Main Street in North's hometown, Philmont, N.Y., thirty miles south of Albany. STEPHEN FERRY/GAMMA LIAISON

The North house on Maple Avenue in Philmont.
STEPHEN FERRY/GAMMA LIAISON

Oliver North with the other members of the Ockawamick
High School cross country team in the spring of 1961. North
is in the back row, fourth from left.
COURTESY: OCKAWAMICK HIGH SCHOOL YEARBOOK

Seventeen-year-old North, shown in his high school yearbook.
NEEFUS PHOTO, COURTESY *LIFE* MAGAZINE

### 1 Killed, 4 Hurt In Erwin Crash

**Naval Academy Group Involved**

**Posts $50 Bail On Driving Count Following Crash**

News clipping of the 1964 car crash in which one Annapolis plebe was killed and North was badly injured. THE LEADER OF CORNING, NY, COURTESY *LIFE* MAGAZINE

North, at right, in his championship bout with James Webb, now Secretary of the Navy. *LUCKY BAG* NAVAL ACADEMY YEARBOOK

North made the academy boxing team despite his injuries. Shown here at upper left, in light jersey. At far right, Coach Emerson Smith.
*LUCKY BAG* NAVAL ACADEMY YEARBOOK

The academy yearbook describes North as a "professional leader" whose ambition was "four stars and a red field," the rank of Commandant of the Marine Corps. *LUCKY BAG* NAVAL ACADEMY YEARBOOK

Midshipman North, shown wearing his dress blues and sabre, center. *LUCKY BAG* NAVAL ACADEMY YEARBOOK

Midshipmen in dress blues outside Bancroft Hall, the main dormitory of the U.S. Naval Academy. NAVAL ACADEMY PHOTO

Marine Lt. North, twenty-five, after finishing a "road sweep" near the village of Cam Lo, Vietnam, six miles south of the Demilitarized Zone, 1969. DON MOORE/*LIFE* MAGAZINE

Lt. Colonel North with Defense Secretary Casper Weinberger in Central America in 1983. P. BOSIO/GAMMA LIAISON

North helped plan the 1986 bombing attack on Libya. The destruction of Qaddafi's main airport is shown above.
REUTERS/BETTMANN NEWSPHOTOS

North assisted in organizing the successful invasion of Grenada. The 82nd Airborne Division drew the sign.
UPI/BETTMANN NEWSPHOTOS

The cruise ship *Achille Lauro* provided the setting for another successful North exploit.
REUTERS/BETTMANN NEWSPHOTOS

Hashemi Rafsanjani, Iran's second most powerful politician, was reportedly in the center of intrigue involving American arms sales to Iran. UPI/BETTMANN NEWSPHOTOS

Carl R. "Spitz" Channell, front left, after he pleaded guilty of evading income taxes in connection with his fund-raising for the contras. AP/ WIDE WORLD PHOTOS

On December 9, 1986, Lt. Colonel Oliver North took the oath before the House Foreign Affairs Committee, but refused to answer any questions concerning Iran or the Contras. UPI/BETTMANN NEWSPHOTOS

Lt. Colonel North, his wife Betsy and youngest daughter Dornin, 6, outside their Great Falls, Virginia, home. BRAD MARKEL/GAMMA LIASION

Stuart North, 16, playing with the family dog while sister Dornin and his mother and father look on. BRAD MARKEL/GAMMA LIAISON

Oliver and Betsy North congratulate daughter Tait, 18, at graduation from high school in Herndon, Virginia. KENNETH JARECKE/CONTACT PRESS IMAGES

Fawn Hall, North's attractive secretary at the NSC.
UPI/BETTMANN NEWSPHOTOS

On July 7, 1987, North takes the oath in front of the Joint Congressional Iran-Contra committees. Senate Chairman Daniel Inouye gestures for North to be seated. UPI/BETTMANN NEWSPHOTOS

Late CIA director, William Casey, flanked by security agents. AP/WIDE WORLD PHOTOS

Defense attorney Brendan Sullivan closely counseled his client Lt. Colonel North, and succeeded in turning the tables on Congressional committee attorneys.
UPI/BETTMANN NEWSPHOTOS

Lt. Colonel North gained national sympathy by revealing that his life had been threatened by notorious international terrorist Abu Nidal. UPI/BETTMANN NEWSPHOTOS

LEADING IRAN-CONTRA WITNESSES: 1) Robert McFarlane, upper left, former National Security Advisor. UPI/BETTMANN NEWSPHOTOS 2) Albert Hakim, an American-Iranian businessman, upper right, was used by North to facilitate the arms sales to Iran. UPI/BETTMANN NEWSPHOTOS 3) General John Singlaub, chairman of the U.S. Council for World Freedom, lower left, testified reluctantly about his activities in the training and support of the contras. UPI/BETTMANN NEWSPHOTOS 4) A pivotal man in the Iran-Contra affair was retired Air Force General Richard Secord, lower right, who managed the private corporations that funneled funds from Iran. UPI/BETTMANN NEWSPHOTOS

5) Retired Air Force Colonel Robert Dutton, upper left, worked closely with Lt. Colonel North in resupplying the contras. UPI/BETTMANN NEWSPHOTOS 6) Assistant Secretary of State Elliott Abrams, upper right, denied knowledge of the diversion of funds. UPI/BETTMANN NEWSPHOTOS 7) Vice Admiral John Poindexter, former National Security Advisor, lower left. UPI/BETTMANN NEWSPHOTOS 8) Attorney General Edwin Meese, lower right. UPI/BETTMANN NEWSPHOTOS

Attorneys for the Joint Committee, John Nields, left, Chief House Counsel; and Arthur Liman, third from left, confer with committee leaders Congressman Lee Hamilton, second left, and Senator Daniel Inouye. NYT PICTURES/GEORGE TAMES

cage waiting to exchange them for American hostages."

Despite the demanding job, North maintained his sense of humor. Since it was usual for him to tackle a hundred pressing assignments a day, he would sometimes answer the phone: "Grand Central Station, Tickets." Still, he always had time for people.

"In the two years he never turned me down when I called or came in," says Peggy Say, sister of Terry Anderson, who was later taken hostage in Iran. "There were times when he called me just to let me know I had a friend, just to let me know there was someone in the world who cared about me and my family."

He was gaining stature, but the true transition from chart-carrier to Ronald Reagan's foreign policy point man came in 1983. In June, NSC chief Clark and his assistant, Robert "Bud" McFarlane, had instituted a Political-Military Affairs Section and named North a deputy director. Despite its ring of authority, the title was less grandiose than it seemed. There was a senior director and two directors above him—even another deputy director alongside.

"But at the NSC, organizational charts meant nothing," recalls Roger Fontaine. "Everybody did what they had to do."

North had learned the power game at Annapolis and in the Marines and he soon filled the work vacuum. He maneuvered his way into key foreign policy assignments, including responsibility for anti-terrorism activity.

It sometimes seemed that Ollie North was in two places at once. The two wristwatches that he often wore, one on each wrist, were a symbol of his endless motion, flying to Central America, then to the Caribbean, then off to Europe.

As a classic workaholic, North picked the most difficult assignments, specializing in what the NSC staff called "hot potatoes," or sensitive issues. As Lieutenant General Singlaub later said: "If there was a loose ball, Oliver North would grab it and run." In addition to his regular job, he was NSC representative on the Intergovernmental Committee for Combatting Terrorism, acting director of a Terrorist Incident Working Group, and secretary for a crisis preplanning group.

During those first two years at the NSC, North was building the expertise that would finally pay off in three spectacular events that he either directed or had an extensive hand in.

In October 1983, a sleepy island in the Caribbean off the main beat of most winter vacationers suddenly became news. Compact, hilly Grenada with a picture-postcard harbor, erupted into violence. There had been two days of ferment on the island since Maurice Bishop, Grenada's Marxist president and most of his Cabinet had been executed in a coup by an extreme pro-Soviet faction that had gained control.

Washington's concerns were manyfold. The island held a strategic location in the center of the Caribbean—a Communist rock-and-dirt "aircraft carrier" at the crossroads of several pro-Western islands. Hundreds of Cuban workers had already half-constructed a modern airport that could double as a military airfield for Russian and Cuban jets.

The island also held a medical school, St. George's, with at least six hundred American students. From intelligence reports, North could visualize the new leaders trying "an Iranian"—taking the students hostage.

North and other NSC staffers immediately went on an around-the-clock emergency basis. He conferred with his new boss, Robert McFarlane, with the CIA, the Defense Department, and the Navy, coordinating the intelligence gathering.

Several times during that crucial week North attended meetings, some chaired by Vice President Bush, in the Crisis Management Room, Number 208 in the Old Executive Office Building. He and Fontaine prepared three intelligence Situation Reports daily. They went to McFarlane, then directly on to the President.

North's assessment was clear. The students' lives were in danger. Never had so many Americans been concentrated in one tinderbox at the same time, available for the taking by terrorists.

"These students were in a very tight spot in Grenada," recalls Roger Fontaine. "I got home the first night at about 2:00 A.M. Ollie didn't get any sleep at all."

North was on the phone to the prime ministers of the nearby Caribbean islands—including Barbados, St. Lucia, Jamaica, Dominica. Like Grenada, all were former British colonies and now independent nations. They agreed with North's assessment. They not only feared hostage-taking but the spread of Cuban and Soviet influence to their own small, vulnerable islands, many without any real defense forces.

At one point North was in contact with a Grenadian in exile in New York who had been planning a local uprising to oust the Communists. From him, he received invaluable intelligence about the island situation.

For days, it was coffee, little food and almost no sleep for Ollie as he helped plan the rescue, racing between his small third floor office in the Executive Office building, the Crisis Management Room, and the Situation Room in the basement of the White House next door. When he did sleep, it was on the couch in his office.

On October 23, the tension increased as North heard another piece of bad news. This one struck at his professional heart. Word came that the Marine barracks in Beirut, Lebanon, had been destroyed, killing 241 men, many of them friends of his.

It was a cowardly atrocity. On the perimeter of Beirut International Airport, a Middle East terrorist had driven a dynamite-laden Mercedes into a cement-block building filled with sleeping leathernecks. In an instant of horror, the explosion ripped out the sides of the three-story structure, which collapsed inward, crushing the men.

The two incidents—the Marine barracks' murder and the Soviet-Cuban takeover in Grenada—were closely related. They were both examples of America's defensive posture, the upshot of a decade of letting the Russians take the lead, then licking our wounds, lamenting our losses, North was afraid. If America was to regain a preeminent position in the eyes of the world and its own citizens, it had to take action, he was convinced. The Reagan Doctrine needed testing.

Unilateral action was possible, but ideally America should have the support of the local nations. That came in a rapid, formal request from the Organization of the Eastern Caribbean States, asking that America help them restore order and democracy in their neighbor island.

North immediately recommended that in order to rescue the six hundred students before they became hostages, that Grenada be invaded by American troops. The invading force, he suggested, should all be Marines, supported by a detachment of Caribbean defense forces. If action was not taken, he feared that the students would be taken hostage, perhaps even killed. McFarlane agreed with the diagnosis, as did the President—except for the idea that it be a Marine exclusive.

It would hardly be a major war, but Grenada could be a symbol of a new American stance. The policy was already being covertly implemented in Central America, Afghanistan, and Angola. Grenada was a chance to take it public.

Prior to the invasion, North was regularly on the phone with Admiral Moreau, the Joint Chiefs of Staff liaison with the NSC, discussing the military and technical aspects. Just promoted from major to lieutenant colonel, North was in the Crisis Management Room in the early morning hours of October 25 when "Operation Urgent Fury" began at 0400 hours.

He had done all his preliminary work. Now all he could do was wait as troops from the Eighty-second Airborne, Navy SEALS, Marines, Army Rangers and a small contingent from the Caribbean nations stormed ashore.

The island was relatively well-fortified for such an apparently innocent spot. The hostile forces, intelligence had learned, were well-armed. The almost 1000 Cuban "construction workers" were also soldiers who quickly grabbed their AK-47 assault rifles at the first sign of the Americans.

Secrecy and surprise, North knew, were the key elements to modern warfare. And unlike the Bay of Pigs, whose landing areas had been leaked to Castro, the strike at Grenada was a true surprise.

The actual invasion had its problems, but it went off relatively smoothly considering the restrictions placed on American troops. They had to exercise "fire control," to be sure innocent civilians were not killed. At one juncture, enemy fire was coming at Marines from a fortified home. Rather than level it, as they were capable of doing, they captured it in a swift bayonet charge, taking some casualties. In all, nineteen Americans died freeing the island.

American troops quickly located the medical students. While the battle was still in progress, the young American men and women were helicoptered off to safety. Barred from the invasion, the American press was initially skeptical of the operation. But when the first students deplaned at Charleston Air Force Base in South Carolina, all doubt vanished.

The first American off the plane bent down and kissed the tarmac. As microphones were thrust into their faces, other students praised the soldiers for their bravery. It was, in a small way, the kind of spontaneous outpouring of patriotism that greeted American victories in World War II. Militarily, it was a minor event, but for many it symbolized a return of American pride after the "malaise" of the Carter Administration, as that former president himself expressed it.

The White House was jubilant, as was the President. For Ollie North, it was an important day for the nation and himself as well. Though still unknown to the public, North had truly come to the attention of the President of the United States. One report stated that the new lieutenant colonel was in the Oval Office with Reagan watching television at the touching moment when the first evacuated student knelt down to embrace American soil.

The briefcase carrier had come into his own.

. . .

With his enhanced reputation, North stretched his power, aided by his superior, NSC chief Robert McFarlane—himself a Marine officer. Increasingly, McFarlane relied on his able young aide. Over the next tense years, North and his group came to be known in Washington as "the cowboys," a backhanded tribute to their willingness to take on tense international problems by cutting through the ponderous federal bureaucracy.

The years 1983–1985 were a time of intense activity. "There were periods of time when we worked two days in every one," North said. "If I had to estimate the number of meetings and discussions and phone calls over that five years, it would surely be in the thousands."

In the words of Neil Livingstone, an anti-terrorist expert, North had become "the most powerful lieutenant colonel in the world."

Terrorism was one of North's key assignments at the NSC. He believed that all anti-terrorist action should be coordinated by the White House, but turf battles at the State Department and the CIA prevented its implementation. He sat helplessly by as Americans were taken hostage in Lebanon. Then, in June 1985, TWA flight 847 was hijacked after leaving the Athens airport.

That tragedy, in which a U.S. Navy diver was murdered, forced the government to put aside their bureaucratic infighting. An inter-agency group to combat terrorism was established. North, who had pressed every intelligence button he could find during the tense seventeen days of the TWA incident, was considered the logical choice for the job.

"The man who was in charge of this anti-terrorist group, Ollie North, was so incredibly overworked that he was putting at least two or three people's horses out of work just to keep up with the jobs that were put to him," recalls Noel Koch, former Pentagon operations planner.

North's anti-terrorist work reached its finest hour during the high seas hijacking of the Mediterranean cruise ship *Achille Lauro* on October 7, 1985. North had no time to celebrate his forty-second birthday when word came into the Situation Room that the Italian ship, with a large number of American passengers aboard, had been seized by four Palestinian terrorists as it approached Port Said, Egypt.

The incident seemed to end abruptly four days later when the hijackers surrendered to Egyptian authorities. In return for releasing the hostages, the Egyptians promised them safe conduct to an undisclosed location. Celebration over the release of the sixty passengers was cut short, however, when it was discovered that the terrorists had murdered a wheelchair-bound American, Leon Klinghoffer, throwing his body into the ocean.

In his crowded office, Ollie North was closely monitoring the seajacking.

"He analyzed the intelligence we were getting," recalls NSC consultant Michael Ledeen, "and he realized that the Egyptians were still holding the terrorists after they said they had let them go."

The Egyptian scam gave the Americans time to formulate a plan.

"Remember Yamamoto?" Navy Commander James Stark, another NSC officer, asked North, reminding him of the time immediately after World War II when the Americans intercepted the plane of escaping Japanese Admiral Yamamoto and forced it down.

Quickly, North formulated a plan. He would gather in the worldwide intelligence and find the terrorists' air route of exit from Egypt. At noon on October 10, President Reagan happened to be visiting Chicago for a tax reform speech when word came to him of North's plan. He conferred with his aides in the private office of a cake factory and quickly approved the idea.

Back in Washington, North threw himself into Operation Yamamoto. He worked with the Navy and the Defense Department, and negotiated the competing demands of State to reach a consensus for the final strategy.

From intelligence, American and Israeli, North learned that a Egyptian commercial 737 airliner would be leaving Cairo that night bound for Algiers. The terrorists had worked out a deal with the Egyptian government.

As the Egyptian airliner left the ground, four American F-14 Navy Tomcats lifted off the deck of the U.S.S. *Saratoga* stationed in the Mediterranean.

The tense moments ticked away into the evening in the White House Situation Room as North and members of the crisis group tried to keep up with and control events. North heard from the Navy. The Tomcats could not find the Egyptian plane. Immediately, Ollie was in secure satellite communication with Israeli intelligence, who located the airliner, then reported back to Washington.

The Israeli information proved accurate. The Tomcats found the Egyptian airline, but when they radioed the pilot to follow, the Egyptian refused.

"Follow us as instructed or we will shoot you down," the F-14 squadron commander ordered.

The 737 quickly radioed "Yes." They accompanied the Navy jets to a NATO base in Sicily, where the plane landed. Italian police quickly surrounded the airliner and arrested the terrorists, who were later placed on trial and sentenced to long prison terms.

"Thank God, we've won one," exclaimed a buoyant Senator Daniel Patrick Moynihan. The New York Daily News exclaimed in a giant headline: WE BAGGED THE BUMS, a front page which soon became a trophy on North's office wall.

It was a major victory against world terrorism and North—still an unknown figure to the public—basked in the appreciation of the President, who now called him "my favorite Marine."

North's work against terrorism was unending. One of the major perpetrators was Libya and its erratic leader Colonel Mohamar Ghadaffi. He had been a continual thorn in America's side, linked to vicious terrorist acts in Europe and the Middle East.

On April 6, 1986, the Libyans pushed the United States—and Ollie North—too far. A Libyan-backed terrorist exploded a bomb in the Belle Disco in West Berlin, a nightclub frequented by American servicemen. One American GI was killed and fifty civilians injured.

It was time to act against Ghadaffi. North, backed by Howard Teicher and Admiral Poindexter, recommended a retaliatory bombing strike against Libya. The President immediately agreed.

This time the Americans were well prepared. Earlier in the year, the National Security Agency (not the NSC), a supersecret electronics intelligence group, had pulled one of its spy satellites out of orbit over Poland and sent it to hover over Libya. It began feeding back invaluable information, which North was able to coordinate through two computers in his office plugged into all U.S. intelligence agencies.

The information signaled the fight to come. In March, 1986, just after the President had ordered the U.S. Navy to cross Ghadaffi's "Line of Death" in the Gulf of Sidra, North's intelligence computers began buzzing. Orders were emanating from Libyan embassies—"People's Bureaus"—throughout the western world: "Cause maximum casualties to U.S. citizens and other Western people."

If the Reagan Doctrine was to mean anything, the response had to be action against the dictator, North knew. Like Grenada, the plan for the Libyan strike was formulated in a matter of days during marathon Crisis Preplanning Group sessions in the Old Executive Office Building. Secrecy was of the essence, North told his colleagues. To prepare the American public for what was about to happen, yet not tip their hand, North and Teicher recommended that parts of the intercepted Libyan terrorist order be released to the media.

A little after 7:00 P.M. Washington time, on the evening of April 14, 1986, United States Air Force F-111 bombers flying from bases in England, and Navy jets launched from a carrier in the Mediterranean, began their attack, first on Libyan coastal defenses, then against Ghadaffi's own headquarters, El Azzizaya, outside Tripoli.

Ghadaffi took vengeance by ordering the murder of an American hostage, Peter Kilburn, in Beirut two days later. But the daring strike, which narrowly missed killing Ghadaffi, frightened the pompous Libyan. His worldwide, sponsored terrorism ground nearly to a halt. The U.S., with the help of a decisive lieutenant colonel, had won another one.

North's boss, NSC chief McFarlane, was one of the few Americans who knew what the young Marine had accomplished. In a letter to North, he unabashedly wrote:

If the world only knew how many times you have kept a semblance of integrity and gumption to U.S. policy, they would make you Secretary of State.

No other accolade could say as much.

*Seven*

---

# Saving the Contras

LIEUTENANT COLONEL OLIVER NORTH, dressed in civvies to appear less conspicuous, stared out the window of the small plane as it wove through the high hills covered with tropical vegetation, then descended into the hot and dusty city of Tegucigalpa, the capital of Honduras, which he had paradoxically code-named "New York."

North was involved in a covert operation in this underdeveloped Central American country where night landings at their main airport were impossible and the phrase "Banana Republic" was born. The mountainous, tropical nation was half the size of Oregon and thirty times poorer.

In fact, the second poorest country in the Western hemisphere.

But because of its geography—it shared a border with Communist Nicaragua—it had become one of the most strategic nations on earth. Thus the presence of Ollie North.

He was whisked through customs by Duane C. Clarridge, a colorful CIA man who sometimes went by the name of "Dewey Maroni." Clarridge was the Agency's division chief for "Operations"—clandestine activities—in Central America.

The CIA man drove North through a teeming, impoverished city of half a million people to the favored section of town. Their destination was a luxurious home, a mansion by Honduran standards, on a street bordered by sweeping high palms and lush, irrigated green lawns. It could have been Miami.

Clarridge was glad to see North. It was the crucial year of 1984 and the CIA chief was worried that the new congressional ban cutting off all money to the Contras meant the end of four years of arduous work spent building a ragtag peasant army into the semblance of a modern fighting force. The Boland Amendment, reluctantly signed into law by the President was to go into effect on October 1, forcing the CIA and the Defense Department to stop their training and supplying of the Nicaraguan resistance movement.

Inside the large house, one of three maintained in Tegucigalpa for the Contras by the CIA, were men even more pleased than Clarridge at the arrival of the "General sent by the President of the United States," as North was called by his hosts. They were the leaders of the FDN, the *Fuerza Democratica Nicaraguense*, the small band that had been struggling for years to win back their country from the Soviet-backed Communist Sandinistas.

The Nicaraguan rebels didn't begin to understand the confusion of American politics, but over the years they had watched anxiously as amendments proposed by Congressman Edward Boland, Democrat of Massachusetts, had slowly eaten away at official American support for their cause.

In December 1981, in the first year of his tenure, President Reagan signed a "finding" permitting covert CIA support for the Contras. But a nervous Congress countered the President's anti-Soviet move by passing the first Boland Amendment on December 21, 1982, barring the CIA and the Defense Department from spending funds to "overthrow the Government of Nicaragua."

The President countered in September 1983

with a second finding, providing "material support and guidance" to the Contras in order to put "pressure on the Sandinista Government" to stop supplying arms to leftist guerrillas in El Salvador and other Central American Countries.

The fight continued: the President versus the Congress. In the summer of 1983, when the CIA helped the Contras mine the Nicaraguan harbors, an angry Congress put a $24-million cap on funds the government could spend on the resistance. But the most recent Boland Amendment, tacked onto a defense appropriation bill at the last moment, was the most severe. Reluctantly signed by a frustrated President Reagan in order to get his larger budget through, it cut off *all* government money for the Contras beginning October 1, 1984.

From 1981, when Reagan took office, until then, the CIA had spent upwards of $80 million organizing the Contras. They were finally beginning to show results, both in training and operations.

After that promising start, the Nicaraguan Contras were fearful that their thousands of homemade soldiers, mainly angry peasants, plus a handful of intellectuals and businessmen risking their lives for a cause, were now going to be deserted by the North American giant.

Clarridge, who North later boasted spoke to President Reagan twice a week, tried to mollify the Contra leaders with North's presence.

"I've come to assure you that the President of the United States is behind you one hundred percent," Ollie told them after he was warmly introduced. "You will not be abandoned."

But having made that pledge, North knew he had to perform a miracle to accomplish it. Without a CIA appropriation, how could he keep the Contra movement alive?

It was essential that the Contras not disband, North was convinced. Never would their army be able to come together again. They were the only viable weapon the U.S. had to contain the Nicaraguan Communists from accomplishing similar Marxist takeovers in neighboring nations.

The assignment to aid the Nicaraguan resistance had been one of McFarlane's earliest upon assuming the reins of the National Security Council from Judge William Clark in October, 1983.

"I told Colonel North to do two things," he recalled. "The first was to be a visible sign of the President's strong personal support, to show the Contras that they would not be forgotten or abandoned, even though we could not provide them with financial support. The second . . . was to help the Contras in their efforts to become a real political movement . . ."

North got his first taste of the Central American "secret" war in June 1983 when he became an integral part of Operation Elephant Herd, a joint CIA-Pentagon supply project for the emerging Contras. Ollie jetted back and forth from Washington to various Central American cities and jungle areas, as $12 million in weapons were delivered to the Nicaraguans. The equipment included Soviet-made weapons captured by Israel from the PLO, and three Cessna O-2 observation planes later equipped with four pods capable of holding twenty-eight rockets.

"He'd shoot down in a two-seater fighter, do business and go back the same day," one Contra supporter recalled.

In the fall of 1983, North got another, more diplomatic introduction to the swamp of Central American politics when the young lieutenant colonel, dressed un-Marine-like in a light casual jacket and chino pants, accompanied the Kissinger Commission on a fact-finding mission through the region. The President's National Bipartisan Commission on Central America, as it was called, was made up of a diverse group including the former secretary of state, the Hispanic mayor of San Antonio, Henry Cisneros, and even the head of the AFL–CIO, Lane Kirkland.

The commission report, delivered early in 1984, echoed North's sentiments—that Communism was primed to take over right in the Northern hemisphere. "The crisis in Central America is acute," the commission warned the nation. "Since the Sandinista victory, Soviets have come around to support Cuba's strategy of armed road to power in Central America."

On another occasion, North found himself in Managua, the capital of Communist Nicaragua, meeting with Sandinista leader Tomas Borge. Despite the enmity between the United States and Nicaragua, the administration recognized the Marxist nation and exchanged diplomats. North was driven to the Sandino Airport by Borge, who kept referring to the colonel as "Comandante."

In Central America, Ollie North thought he was back in Vietnam again. Not in a military sense: he was sure that the Marines and the disaffected Nicaraguans, within and outside their country, could easily take the territory back despite Soviet arms. The parallel was in the lack of American resolve, he feared. In Nicaragua, America had once again played "Uncle Sucker."

President Jimmy Carter had supported the Sandinista revolution, hoping for a democratic outcome once the dictator, Anastosio Somoza, was ousted. The CIA had even backed the Sandinistas with cash, and between 1979 and 1981, Carter and Congress had given the new revolutionary government $118 million in economic aid, unwittingly helping them to build thirty-six new military bases, to bring in 2000 Cuban military advisors, and to arm themselves with Russian tanks, 152 mm. howitzers, anti-aircraft guns and the deadly helicopter gunships.

North knew it was another Cuba, all over again. Back in the late 1950s, as North learned at the Naval War College, Castro had convincingly posed as a "democrat" whose true heroes were Abraham Lincoln and George Washington. As with "Danny" Ortega in Nicaragua, his was a false face put on for the gullible American public, who actually backed Castro's takeover. Not long after, Castro revealed that he was a Soviet-supported Marxist Leninist.

Now, the Nicaraguans were confessing as well. A few months after assuming power, the Sandinista leader, Daniel Ortega traveled to Cuba, where he saluted "Comandante and Comrade Fidel Castro," praising Che Guevara as a hero. His brother, Defense Minister Humberto Ortega, spelled it out succinctly: "Marx-ism-Leninism is the scientific doctrine that guides our revolution."

As McFarlane had indicated, President Reagan was firmly behind North in his new assignment. In a Joint Session of Congress, the President had reminded the American people:

> El Salvador is nearer to Texas than Texas is to Massachusetts. Nicaragua is just as close to Miami, San Antonio, San Diego and Tucson as those cities are to Washington where we are gathered tonight. . . . Are democracies required to remain passive while threats to their security and prosperity accumulate?

Now in 1984, sitting in a living room in Honduras with the anxious, expatriate Nicaraguans, North was more worried than he appeared to the resistance leaders. He too feared that Congress would again become passive in the face of the Communist threat. But he also knew that the President had no such intentions. Ollie North, the good soldier, had just been given his marching orders.

Singlehandedly, he had to save the Contras.

. . .

On the Boland cut-off date, October 1, 1984, Room 302 of the Old Executive Office Building, staffed by Lieutenant Colonel Oliver L. North, his secretary Fawn Hall, and another assistant, became the spiritual, and sometimes operational, nerve center of the Nicaraguan resistance.

When North moved into his job at the end of September 1984, the CIA-Central American Task Force chief reported: "There was only one point in the apparatus who was functioning and who seemed to be able and was interested and was working on the process, and that was Ollie North."

North's first step was to check out the legality of his new assignment. Could he and the NSC operate on behalf of the Contras despite the congressional ban?

The Boland Amendment had prohibited any government agency "involved in intelligence activities" from aiding the Contras. Specifically, this meant the CIA and the Defense Department.

The CIA had quickly moved to obey the new law. Dropping out of the Contra picture, they sent a stern warning to their agents: "Field stations are to cease and desist with actions which can be construed to be providing any type of support, either direct or indirect, to the various entities with whom we dealt under the program."

The only permissible contact with the Contras, Langley insisted to its men, was for the purpose of "collecting positive and counterintelligence information of interest to the United States."

North's question remained: Was the NSC covered by Boland? Was it legal for North to be helping the Contras out of the White House—or next door, in his Executive Office Building suite? North thought so, as did the President. North believed that as an arm of the White House, the NSC was covered by the President's constitutional control of foreign affairs.

The argument was supported by the President's Intelligence Oversight Board, which concluded that (1) "the NSC is not covered by the prohibition; (2) None of Lt. Colonel's activities during the past year constitutes a violation of the Boland Amendment."

Legal or not, the White House ruling couldn't conjure up the millions needed to keep the Contras alive. The NSC might have power, but it had no money. Only Congress could appropriate that.

North and the President decided that the only way to keep the Contras alive was to go *outside* the government for funds. There were two logical choices—the American public and friendly foreign governments.

Meanwhile, the small suite on the third floor became a makeshift operational command center for the Resistance. Once again, Lieutenant Colonel North was a Marine officer, struggling to keep the Contras militarily on target.

David Halevy, a journalist who became close to North, describes a visit to North's office during this hectic period.

"It was not unusual to be sitting in his office in the Old Executive Office Building and to hear Fawn Hall interrupt him with an urgent phone call from 'the boys down south,'" Halevy recounts. "North would occasionally admonish the visitor to 'forget everything you're about to hear,' and then without hesitation, pick up the telephone and bark commands to his field operators in Central America.

"One of them joked that North had come to be known as 'Mr. Sir' because whenever he got a call from North, the field operator's end of the conversation went something like this: 'Yes, sir. Yes, sir. Affirmative, sir. Right, sir. Okay, goodbye, sir."

Operations were sometimes hamstrung because of the CIA, which feared it might be breaking the Boland Amendment. At one point, this crippled a Contra plan to take out the deadly Hind-D Soviet helicopter gunships. FDN leader Adolfo Calero desperately needed information for a planned raid and asked North for help. In November of 1984, North wrote a memo to McFarlane explaining that earlier on he had forwarded intelligence information on the helicopters from the CIA national intelligence officer for Latin America to Calero. He wanted permission to continue.

That same day, Calero flew from Miami to Washington to see North about the helicopter raid. But when the CIA people heard he was coming, they refused to meet with North and his FDN colleague.

The Contra movement was highly personal to North. He kept a shoebox full of photographs of the "freedom fighters" who were bivouacked along the Rio Coco. On his office wall, behind his desk, was a picture of a young Miskito Indian girl, a member of the tribe that was literally driven from their homes by the Sandinistas and sent to relocation camps and into forced labor.

"Villagers were arbitrarily shot when the government soldiers first invaded the villages," relates a geography professor from the University of California who had visited the village in 1980. "Others were killed during the weeks of occupation, confinement, torture and interrogation."

It was obvious that North felt deeply about his mission. "In his trips to Central America, he spent a lot of time in the Contra camps," a former NSC staffer recalled, "and the pictures he brought home were not of military forces, but of women and children and the terrible conditions they were living in. . . . He personalized it, internalized it."

Not only did North try to inspire and direct the Contras, he sometimes had to restrain them from military actions they were not ready for. One time, he admonished Contra leader Adolfo Calero not to launch an attack inside Nicaragua. Calero agreed. But when North found out the raid had taken place anyway, he exhibited a temper. The Contras had lost their only workable helicopter on the Northern Front.

Getting other helicopters, guns, food, medicine and uniforms—everything needed to fight a war—became North's one man responsibility. He rapidly started to build an organization around him, a group of trusted private citizens who could raise money and who had the ability to buy munitions and resupply the desperate army, which was growing rapidly as Sandinista oppression increased inside Nicaragua.

North came to rely on two major players on his team. Both were retired generals with experience that counted. Army Lieutenant General

Singlaub, former U.S. ground commander in Korea, had locked horns with President Jimmy Carter and won.

When Singlaub heard the President was considering withdrawing U.S. troops from South Korea—which could have triggered a Communist invasion of that strategic country—he threatened to resign and make a public statement. He approached Senator John Glenn of Ohio, the celebrated astronaut and former Marine colonel, who gathered a group together in the Senate. Quietly, they persuaded Carter that his plan was rash.

Singlaub, a gaunt-faced, serious man, now took on a dual role for North. He flew to Asia and returned with a $2-million donation from some people in Taiwan. Simultaneously, he became a munitions broker for the Contras, entering the giant world market to secure the arms they needed. Later, Singlaub made several trips to the Contra front and arranged to have former CIA and military men work as "trainers" for the raw troops.

The second player was retired Air Force Major General Richard V. Secord, whom North had first met at the NSC. A West Point graduate in his early fifties, the stocky, taciturn—even highly secretive—man had already spent half his life in covert actions. He had flown two hundred secret combat missions in Vietnam, helping the CIA fight a clandestine war in Laos. He had been the Air Force's advisor to the Shah of Iran and in 1981, was named chief Middle East advisor on arms sales to Defense Secretary Caspar Weinberger. Like North, he was a courageous man, having won a Distinguished Flying Cross for a dangerous rescue mission in the Congo.

Secord had the credentials that were essential to North's task. He could raise money, buy munitions, and most important—now that the CIA was out of the picture—develop a desperately needed air supply system for the Contras.

At that time, supply for the Contra operation was catch-as-catch-can. Some of the rebel commanders were a thirty days' mule-march from their base camps. The soldiers had so little food that they sometimes dropped off the supplies and ate the mules.

"They were running out of mules," Secord recalls. "It didn't take a Napoleon to figure it out. It's an age-old problem, one I've dealt with my whole career."

North decided to arrange a meeting between his two most important Contra aides: Secord and Adolfo Calero, a tall, white-haired man with unruly features who looked more like a Coca-Cola bottling executive—which he had been in

Nicaragua—than a guerilla leader. Fluent in English, Calero had been active in the anti-Somoza strikes that forced the dictator out. When the Sandinista Communists stole the revolution, Calero went into exile and was now the political director of the FDN.

The three men held their rendezvous at the Miami International Airport Hotel, a five-story oasis inside the airport built for people in a hurry. The marble-floored lobby was on the upper level of the airport's Concourse E and less than a minute's walk from the terminal gates. It was perfect for Ollie North, who hadn't a minute to waste.

In one of the hotel's 260 soundproofed rooms, the men talked all night. Calero detailed the difficulties of fighting a war against the Sandinistas, who were receiving $250 million a year from the Russians, along with skilled Cuban and Soviet advisors and potent equipment. The Contras not only needed arms, they had to develop a workable air-drop supply system. Would Secord help them with both?

Secord was neither ignorant of the Contra activity nor was he a neophyte in the arms business. He listened with two motives in mind. Now that he was retired from the service he was an American businessman who needed to make money for his firm, Stanford Technology, which he ran with his partner, Albert Hakim, an Iranian-American. And he wanted to help out his country.

He promised North that with his contacts around the world he could secure the best prices for the Contra arms and supplies and still make a profit for himself.

"I'll try it," he told Calero and North at the end of the long night. Then staring hard at Ollie, he added: "But you're going to have to raise millions to support this."

North assured him. Somehow he would get the money.

.  .  .

Before North and Secord came into the picture, the air supply system to the Contras fighting inside Nicaragua was hopeless. One pilot explained that they were able to fly into a war zone only when the weather was too bad for the Sandinista pilots to take off. Even then they often failed to make radio contact with their own people on the ground.

"The Contra air arm was a laugh," said Secord, "It was seven guys, none of whom had the skills or the airplanes capable of flying missions."

The new team headed by North began a reorganization of the resupply system. Secord brought in a private airline firm to run the operation on a commercial basis, with Fairchild C-123K cargo planes instead of the older C-47s. The 123s were faster and could fly lower, avoiding radar detection. The covert resupply project was now being administered by experts who flew with doctored flight manifests that would not arouse the suspicion of the Federal Aviation Administration or the Central American countries.

It was a complex operation, but it was soon running on a regular basis. Planes picked up munitions around the world, including Dulles International Airport, where the pilots were outfitted with proper maps, weather reports and the latest intelligence on Nicaraguan air defenses. The supplies were dropped off at the Aguacate base in Honduras, at the Ilopango airbase in El Salvador, and at a secret 6,520-foot airstrip built in Costa Rica on ranch land donated by a Contra supporter, an American named John B. Hull. Near the Nicaraguan border, the crude airstrip supplied the Southern Front. The operation was not elegant, but it was working.

Coded communications between North, Secord and other members of the team were handled through top-secret KL-43 encryption devices that North had obtained through the NSC.

Munitions came pouring in from Singlaub, Secord, and another supplier, a retired lieutenant colonel. In one shipment, North recorded, they received 8,910 grenades (at a cost of $84,645), 1,000 Rocket Propelled Grenades (for $265,000), and 3,245 pounds of C-4 plastic explosive ($96,000).

Things were progressing, but as Secord had reminded North, everything had to be paid for. Once again, *Comandante Norte,* as some of the Contras called him, began another enterprise: raising the $35- to $50-million-a-year the Contras needed to prosecute even a small war to regain their nation's independence.

So much money was required that it had to come from many outside sources—from any reasonable donor except the almost paralyzed American government.

The first and largest source was friendly foreign governments. The most generous was Saudi Arabia, who through their ambassador to Washington, Prince Bandar bin Sultan, donated $1 million a month, about one-third the budget needed to keep the Contras at a subsistence level. That, North reminded those involved, would only ensure a slow, painful defeat.

A half dozen other nations gave as well, but it

was soon clear that to successfully support a resistance, North's people would have to turn to
the American public, particularly to wealthy
contributors.

The money was solicited by a number of non-
profit organizations, including General Singlaub's Worldwide Anti-Communist League and
Carl Channell's National Endowment for the
Preservation of Liberty. Funds from these
groups and from such large contributors as beer
magnate Joseph Coors, heiress Ellen St. John
Garwood, and others, found their way to the
Contras through special bank accounts in Swit-
zerland, Miami, and the Caribbean.

North solicited no money personally, but he
stimulated others with his eloquent slide show,
which revealed the danger of the Soviet pene-
tration into Central America.

"The Soviets are outspending us in our own
hemisphere on a ratio of about five to one,"
North explained, showing a slide of a Russian
warship cruising the Caribbean. "Sixteen miles
off the coast of Louisiana, the Kiev battle group
deployed for a refueling and replenishment exercise."

North then flashed a photo of Soviet subma-
rines based in Cuba, reminding his audience
that in the early days of World War II, Hitler

was able to sink almost half the ships traveling to Europe with German U-boats.

He then switched to Nicaragua, to a giant Soviet airbase being built at Punta Huete. "It is the largest airfield south of the Rio Grande, bigger than Andrews Air Force Base, capable of launching and receiving any aircraft in the Soviet inventory," he told a rapt audience. He then moved to photos of Soviet T-55 tanks, 150 of which had been given to the Sandinistas, along with armored personnel carriers, "numbering over 330."

Much of the Soviet equipment had come in surreptitiously so as not to alert the Americans, North explained. With a wry smile, he flashed a slide of the Soviet-made MI-8HIP helicopters. "They were delivered originally as agricultural support equipment," North told his audience. "It shows some of the unique agricultural support uniforms, and of course the party emblem next to the agricultural rocket-launchers on the side of the aircraft."

North's detailed, impassioned insight into the Soviet threat near home helped to loosen the pockets of donors. Some openly commented on how strange it was that one energetic young Marine was doing the work that should be done by the entire American government, with its unlimited resources.

The money came in, in millions. Saudi Arabia increased its donation from $1 million to $2 million a month. Other contributions were much smaller, but still significant, and particularly satisfying to North.

General Secord recounts a story of one unusual supporter. Robert Owen, a liaison man for the movement—now labeled "Project Democracy" by North—who had been sent to New York by Secord to pick up some money for the Contras at a bank. But it was a Jewish holiday and the bank, ostensibly an Israeli one, was closed. Owen called back to Secord, who then dispatched him down to Chinatown, to a Chinese food market. There, an old man lifted his pants leg and from his socks extracted a wad of $100 bills—$9,500 in all—and gave them to Owen.

From all sources, North reported to McFarlane, from July 1984, when the federal funds for the Contras had run out, until April 9, 1985, the FDN had received $24.5 million and had spent $17,145,594. The balance book looked good, but the small ragtag army was growing and was beginning to swallow considerably larger amounts of money for sustenance and arms. North recommended to his boss that the FDN "seek additional funds from the current donors ($15–20M) which will allow the force to grow to 30–35,000."

Not long after, in the summer of 1985, the Congress—perhaps fearful of being blamed for the Sovietization of Central America—decided it was best to waffle on the Contras. North cheered when in August, they voted $27 million in "humanitarian" aid, not to be administered by either the CIA or the Defense Department. It wouldn't buy guns or planes, but it would at least feed his people.

Still, North was impatient for a substantial congressional appropriation of several hundred million to match the Russian investment in Sandinista Nicaragua. There was, as Secord commented, never enough money.

On March 31, 1986, even the $27 million in humanitarian assistance ran out. North was now faced with an even greater financial dilemma. All the donors and foreign nations had been tapped to the limit. North became increasingly uneasy, angered by the Congress, and impatient for help.

His impatience was exceeded by that of only one man, the President of the United States. Despite his vaunted power as "the leader of the Free World," he had been stymied by a minor amendment attached to an appropriations bill.

In May 1986, almost two years since Colonel North had begun his holding action in Nicaragua, the President paced the Oval Office seeking a solution to the steady, incremental power of the Sandinistas, who—with the Cubans—were threatening the security of the Western hemisphere. If Central America fell, Mexico could be next. America would then be faced with a bloody war of enormous proportions on the Rio Grande. It was best, Reagan was sure, to stop Communism in Central America now.

He intended to propose a $100-million appropriation from Congress for the next fiscal year to fund the Contras. It was enough to keep them going, and it would legitimize American aid, from both the CIA and the Defense Department. But not everyone around the White House thought the appropriation would pass.

The President's fallback had always been Colonel North. Reagan anticipated that the young Marine he so admired could hold the Contras together until more substantial—government—help was on its way. But how much longer could the Marine hold out?

If Congress refused to help, there was only one other possible route, the President decided.

On May 15, 1986, President Reagan called Admiral Poindexter into the Oval Office. "I am really serious," he told his NSC chief. "If we can't move the Contra package before June 9,

I want to figure out a way to take action unilaterally to provide assistance."

What the President was thinking of was using his power as commander in chief to provide direct military assistance to the resistance, without the approval of Congress.

The next day, Admiral Poindexter wrote a memo to his staff, including Ollie North, on the subject. "The fact remains," Poindexter said, "that the President is ready to confront the Congress on the Constitutional question of who controls foreign policy."

The NSC chief laid out the President's thinking on the subject, adding that the Contras had become desperate for money. The President, Poindexter explained, had read a book edited by an Israeli terrorist expert and "was taken with the examples of presidential actions in the past without congressional approval."

As students of American history know, the list is long. Jefferson concluded a deal with Napoleon to buy the Louisiana Territory for $15 million before Congress gave its approval; John Tyler concluded a secret deal to annex Texas without Congress; James K. Polk sent General Zachary Taylor to the Mexican border and began the Mexican War without congressional authorization.

The prime example, the President knew, was

Abraham Lincoln. Without congressional approval or a declaration of war, Lincoln called for volunteers to fight the Civil War; established a naval blockade of southern ports; suspended habeus corpus; put enemy sympathizers in Army jails without trial; and used his powers as commander in chief to free the slaves.

In the case of the Contras, there was Clause 506A of the Foreign Assistance Act. It permitted the President, without Congress, to send emergency military assistance to any country he wished. All he had to do was recognize the resistance as the legitimate Nicaraguan government, then grant it the full backing of the American armed forces.

Would he do it? There were those around the White House who thought the President might if Congress continued to bedevil him on foreign policy in general, and the Reagan Doctrine in particular.

But meanwhile, the lieutenant colonel who was responsible for keeping the resistance alive sat in his office on the third floor of the Old Executive Office Building studying the Poindexter memo.

More than anyone, North knew that the admiral had not exaggerated the Contra's dire need for money. But North had a plan. He had only barely started its execution, but he knew it was promising.

If the Congress did not act—soon—Lieutenant Colonel Oliver North felt he had no choice but to carry it out if he was to fulfill his mission for the President.

---

# Eight

# Mission to Tehran: Innocence Lost

THE DATE WAS MAY 25, 1986.

The mission was perhaps the most improbable of the many Ollie North had undertaken in his years of service to his country. Seated in a black-painted, specially-equipped Israeli Air Force 707 taking off from Tel Aviv Airport at 8:30 in the morning, the lieutenant colonel was accompanied by a unique "platoon" of men.

On the plane with North were Bud McFarlane, former National Security Advisor to the President and head of the mission; George Cave, former CIA expert on the Mideast; Howard Teicher, Ollie's nominal boss as director of the NSC's Political-Military Affairs section; Amiram Nir, an advisor on terrorism to Israeli Prime Minister Shimon Peres; and a CIA communicator in touch with his opposite number on the ground in Tel Aviv. From there, the electronic line ran to the White House Situation Room and to President Reagan.

Although this was an official U.S. Government operation, only two of the men—North and Teicher—were government employees. Aside from the Israeli, the others were private American citizens. The entire team were traveling under false names, carrying Irish passports. Cave was "O'Neil" and North was masquerading as a "Mr. Goode."

It could be a scene from a film except that the script was too fanciful and the lives of several Americans, the hostages held by the Islamic Hezbollah in Lebanon, were dependent on the success of the mission.

Retired Major General Richard Secord—code named "Copp"—who had handled arrangements for the team in Israel from May 22 on, was not on board. Secord, a stocky, taciturn former Air Force advisor to the Shah of Iran and North's associate on the Contra supply, had been called in by North to help coordinate the Iranian Initiative. Nor was another key player, Albert Hakim, Secord's partner and the American-Iranian businessman who had acted as an intermediary, on the plane.

But the others were on their way to Tehran, supposedly to meet with "moderate" elements of the Iranian government interested in a dialogue leading to a rapprochment between the two countries.

The United States had not exchanged a civil word with Iran since November 1979 when radical students—with the blessings of the Ayatollah—seized the United States Embassy and held fifty-two Americans hostage for 444 days. In April 1980, when eight Americans died in President Carter's ill-fated attempt to rescue the hostages, North was in the Mediterranean with a Third Marine amphibious assault unit. A "debacle in the desert," North said of the failed Carter attempt.

Khomeini, who had already once humbled the American giant, appeared to be doing it again. The script was different, but Iran had now seized still more hostages, this time indirectly through their Hezbollah followers in Beirut. In effect, the Iranians were forcing the Americans to deal with them surreptitiously if the lives were to be saved.

Iran's goal was simple: to secure enough American arms to fight the continuing, bleeding war against Iraq. They had bought munitions from nineteen nations, but the American aid was crucial: they needed spare parts and replacements for the massive amount of equipment, including F-14 fighters, that the Defense Department had sold the Shah before he was deposed in 1979.

The upcoming meeting in Tehran was not the first between the two countries. Secret conferences had been held in Europe. In October of 1985, Vice Admiral Poindexter had met the Iranians in Geneva while North had attended three meetings in London and Germany. And two years before, the CIA and Khomeini's secret police had informally cooperated.

The CIA had continued to operate in Iran after the fall of the Shah and were in possession of a list of KGB agents within the Tudeh, or Communist party of Iran. The list was turned over to Khomeini's people, who acted swiftly. The Tudeh party was outlawed, the party leaders were arrested, and some two hundred Communist suspects were executed. Shortly after, eighteen Soviet diplomats were expelled from the country.

North didn't doubt the Ayatollah's anti-Communism. That country, he knew, was secretly helping the Afghan resistance fighters as well. But that didn't make Iran a friend of the United States or reduce the danger of their trip. North, not one to hesitate out of fear, faced the journey to Tehran with the same resolve he had showed in storming a ridge in Quangtri. But with the understanding that he was engaged in an equally hazardous outing.

The rendezvous in Iran could be a trap, a chance to seize the negotiators, adding prominent Americans to their roster of hostages.

North hid that anxiety, taking along a small gift, a chocolate cake in the shape of a key, a delicacy he had bought in a kosher Tel Aviv bakery. The American delegation had brought other gifts as well, including six .357 Blackhawk magnum revolvers in presentation boxes. But the real "key" North and his colleagues were carrying was a pallet of spare parts for Hawk anti-aircraft missiles parts sequestered in the cargo bay of the Israeli 707.

When the American team arrived at Tehran's Medrabad Airport, which was also an Iranian Air Force base, they could have been mistaken for a group of anonymous tourists waiting for an indifferent guide. The high Iranian officials they expected—as arranged by Iranian go-between and arms merchant Manuchehr Ghorbanifar—were not on hand to greet them.

They waited an hour and a half before anyone arrived to escort them to the site of the talks, the Independence Hotel—formerly the Hilton—at the airport. Like tourists suspected of running out on a bill, their passports were confiscated.

North chafed at the cool reception but he had no one to complain to. The visit, though authorized by President Reagan, was secret. They had to accept whatever accommodations they could get. That included not only adequate hotel rooms but the conspicuous presence of burly, mustached Iranian security men as well. North had the feeling that they were not just there as "protection" against extremists. The Americans were under virtual house arrest. The "Great Satan," as the Islamic fundamentalists called the United States, was not in the driver's seat.

Ollie North and McFarlane had come to Tehran with several goals: to stop Iranian terrorism around the world; to open a diplomatic initiative with this strategic country between Russia and the Mideast oil supply; and third—and most frustrating—to get back the hostages taken by pro-Iranians in Lebanon. Thus far, the might of the United States and its ally, Israel, had succeeded in freeing only one, Episcopal priest Benjamin Weir.

He was released in September 1985 after the delivery of TOW anti-tank missiles to Iran by the Israelis, a transfer that had been approved by the White House. Five other Americans— Reverend Lawrence Jenco; journalist Terry An-

derson; American Hospital official David Jacobsen; American University Dean Thomas Sutherland; and the CIA head-of-station in Beirut,
William Buckley—were still in their hands. Reports indicated that all were alive except Buckley, who had been savagely tortured and
murdered.

Israel was not new to secret negotiations with
Iran. They had begun their own Iranian Initiative back in 1979, a turnabout in foreign policy
that had emerged out of a keen sense of survival. Since Iraq was a powerful Arab enemy of
the Jewish state, Iraq's enemy—Iran—had to be
favored in the Gulf War even though Iran hated
the beleagured state.

Not only had the Israelis made a geopolitical
decision and backed it with the sale of $50 mil-
lion in arms to Iran, they were determined to
bring America around to the same viewpoint.
They could hardly continue to sell vital arms to
Iran without having them replaced by the
United States.

Ollie North was, as usual, in the center of the
drama. At a breakfast at the Hay-Adams Hotel
in Washington with Neil Livingstone, anti-terrorist expert and adjunct professor at Georgetown University, Ollie North explained
his—and the administration's—rationale. Much

of it was based on secret information about Soviet intentions.

North told Livingstone that the Soviets expected a replay of the Russian army's disastrous Tannenberg campaign during World War I. The Czarist general staff had planned a "final offensive" to knock Germany out of the war. Instead they saw their forces shattered, with losses ten-to-one against the enemy's, North explained. The Russians never recovered from that debacle, which had sown the seeds of the Bolshevik revolution.

American intelligence had since learned that Iran intended to do the same in its war with Iraq—to launch a "final offensive" to destroy the enemy. But, North told Livingstone, Iraq is considerably stronger than anyone thought. They would badly defeat the Iranians, repeating the lesson of Tannenberg.

The Soviets would then rush to exploit the weakened Iranian regime. Russian troops were massed on the long Iranian border and special *Spetsnaz* sabotage and terrorist troops were to be introduced into Iran along with six hundred KGB agents to create chaos. Together, they would prepare the ground for a Communist coup in Tehran once the Iranian army had been crushed. Moscow's allies would take over the government and "request" Soviet military assistance, the same scenario played out in the invasion of Afghanistan.

In the event that this Soviet plan failed, the alternative called for a Soviet-backed revolt in Iranian Azerbaijan, which would immediately call for help from Moscow.

The Soviet plan was based on American impotence in the area. For public relations reasons, the United States could not openly show any friendship for Iran. The terrorist state had alienated too many Americans for that. But if the NSC staff could make secret contact with Iran, they might offer friendship despite the recriminations of the past, North and McFarlane suggested. First, there had to be a return of the hostages, a "hurdle" to be overcome if the Iranians were to expect better relations.

President Reagan had agreed with Ollie's thinking. Thus the trip to Tehran.

The Iranians had, of course, written the script for the meeting. The Americans were told that there was domestic opposition to the "Old Man," as Ghorbanifar called Khomeini. The ostensibly more moderate, pro-Western, group was headed by the speaker of the parliament, Hofatolislam Hashemi Rafsanjani. North and the others had come to meet his people, and perhaps, only perhaps, the man himself.

They had already showed some of their bona

fides, the Iranians claimed. Terrorism against Americans had slackened only because of their efforts against the hardliners around Khomeini. The "final offensive," which would have been disastrous, had been postponed by the "pragmatists" who were only waiting for the right time to take over and purge Khomeini's hand-chosen successor, Ayatollah Hussein Ali Montazeri. In addition Rafsanjani had personally intervened to gain the freedom of the last four hostages from the TWA kidnapping in June of 1985.

By May 25, 1986, the time of the crucial Tehran trip, North was already experienced in the hostage crisis. As NSC point man on military-political affairs, terrorism was one of his major assignments. Though not as crippling to the operation of the White House as it had been in Carter's days, the taking of American hostages greatly troubled President Reagan. He seemed to bleed more over that than virtually any other presidential issue.

The chief executive had made the hostage release a top priority. Ollie, ever aware of his superior's needs, had been on the assignment for eighteen months. North, too, felt strongly for the plight of the hostages and their families—perhaps too much for a man of action, some thought. But not Peggy Say, sister of hostage Terry Anderson.

"None of the others in the administration ever showed the consideration he did," she says. "When David Jacobsen was released without Terry, Ollie was so upset he cried."

As the *Achille Lauro* incident showed, North had the skill to deal with terrorists. He privately favored the Israeli method: swift, person-to-person retaliation, which the Soviets had already shown to be effective. When Russian diplomats were seized in Beirut by Arab extremists, the KGB located the kidnappers. After torturing and executing them, the KGB delivered the dismembered bodies to terrorist headquarters. No Russian has been bothered in Lebanon since.

North was anxious to use his own Marine tactics to hunt down and kill the terrorists one by one. But he was hamstrung, forced to play by the restraints of the Washington political game.

The arms sales to Iran—whether for a new opening to that strategic, oil-rich country or for the release of the hostages, or both—was first broached back in July, 1984. David Kimche, director general of the Israeli Foreign Ministry, mentioned it to NSC Advisor Robert McFarlane, implying that America might trade the munitions for hostages. Three hostages had already been taken in Lebanon but McFarlane brushed aside the idea as inconsistent with American policy.

The actual beginnings were reportedly made by Theodore B. Shackley, former American CIA chief in Laos and No. 2 man in the Operations, or clandestine, CIA section. An oft-mentioned future candidate for Director, the tall, fair-skinned operator in his late fifties was respected in Langley, where, in small whispers, he was referred to as "The Blond Ghost."

In November of that same year, Shackley, at the suggestion of the Israelis, met with Iranian middleman Ghorbanifar, who was living in Europe. They discussed the possibility of ransoming the American hostages for cash. Ghorbanifar, who was to become a key player in the story, had been variously described as being close to the Iranian power center, as a CIA agent, and even as a double agent working for MOSSAD, the Israeli secret service.

Shackley and Ghorbanifar met several times, during which the Iranian hinted that American arms would be welcome. Under the right circumstances, his people in Iran might convince the Hezbollah extremists to release some hostages.

The next threads of the Iranian Initiative are still tangled but most believe the chain continued from Shackley to his friend, Michael Ledeen, an anti-terrorist consultant to the National Security Council. Ledeen was dispatched to see the Israelis, who had already decided they preferred Iran to win the Gulf War. McFarlane and North sent Ledeen to Europe, where he met in secret with Israeli Prime Minister Peres, who convinced him that arms to Iran was the West's best hope in the area. And—it might bring home the hostages from Lebanon.

Ollie's first thought was to use money instead of arms as ransom. He worked out a plan for a $4-million payment in return for all the hostages, calling on an offer from tycoon H. Ross Perot to put up $2 million. North planned to use American DEA narcotics agents as clandestine go-betweens. One fanciful idea was contemplated: to pay the ransom in chemically-treated money that disintegrated in seventy-two hours, long after the hostages were home. But when North's Lebanese go-between disappeared, the cash-ransom plan was dropped.

Neither North nor McFarlane initially favored the arms-for-friendship, or arms-for-hostages idea. But there seemed to be no alternative if the Americans were to be taken out of Lebanon alive—a White House "must." In a series of meetings in Europe between Ledeen, Ghorbanifar and Israeli officials, the question of an arms ransom was suggested by Ghorbanifar.

On August 30, 1985, Israel—now with America's approval—shipped 100 TOW anti-tank missiles to Tehran, followed by a larger second shipment of 408 TOWs on September 14. The following day, the first hostage, Benjamin Weir, was released. The plan, as distasteful as it was to North, seemed to be working.

In Room 302 of the Executive Office Building, an encouraged lieutenant colonel sat with John Poindexter and Robert McFarlane. Elated at release, he laid out the plan to get back the other hostages and simultaneously open a diplomatic door to Iran.

The man to help him do the job, he suggested, was the same one who had proven so resourceful in the Contra effort, retired Major General Secord. As a private citizen, Secord could—unlike the CIA—set up a network that would be immune to congressional oversight. Without *total* secrecy, North stressed, the plan would be exposed and collapse before it was tested.

North's superiors agreed, and Secord began the Iránian phase of his extraordinary worldwide covert operation. The general planned to work with his business partner, Albert Hakim, an Iranian-American businessman with excellent contacts in America, the Mideast, and ostensibly in Iran.

The project was so sensitive that in the beginning even top government officials were excluded. Secord and Hakim created such a clandestine aura that they were able to convince John Kelly, the American ambassador to Lebanon, to cooperate without informing his boss, Secretary of State George Shultz.

Secrecy within the NSC, with its tight relationship with the Oval Office, is not new. It has long rankled bureaucrats in other agencies. When Henry Kissinger was President Nixon's National Security Advisor, he conducted secret diplomacy with both China and the Soviet Union, establishing a "back channel" that totally bypassed the angered State Department.

Defense Secretary Weinberger—who was to complain that he first learned of North's activity from foreign intelligence—was not the first defense leader cut out. In Kissinger's day, the Chairman of the Joint Chiefs of Staff had to infiltrate a spy into the NSC to learn what was going on.

North had been able to maintain total secrecy, but the next step in the Iranian Initiative faltered anyway. On November 17, 1985, Ollie was in his Executive Office Building office one evening monitoring reports from the Geneva Summit, where President Reagan and Mikhail Gorbachev were discussing nuclear survival. North's problems were smaller but just as pressing. The Israelis were making another Hawk shipment to Tehran, which—if one could trust the Iranians—would result in the release of more hostages.

Suddenly, North was called to the phone. It was from New York, from Israeli Foreign Minister Rabin, who was visiting his embassy. Rabin maintained phone security, only telling North that there was a problem with the shipment. Could he come to New York?

"Yes, Mr. Minister. I'll be there in less than two hours."

The second he hung up, the phone rang again. It was Bud McFarlane, interrupting his work at the Geneva Summit.

"Ollie, this is Bud. You're going to get a call from Prime Minister Rabin."

"I just did," North responded.

"You go take care of the problem," McFarlane said and hung up.

In New York, North met with Rabin, who outlined the problem in detail. A chartered Israeli plane was at the Lisbon airport loaded with a cargo of supposed "oil drilling" machines. Actually, they were Hawk missiles bound for Tehran. The Portuguese had guessed that the manifest was false. Afraid to become involved, they were refusing to clear the plane for takeoff. The Israeli opening to Iran was grounded.

This was a job for Secord, North decided.

Ollie immediately called Secord in Florida and asked him to fly to Lisbon to settle the mess. Secord, who was busy with the Contra resupply work, was reluctant. "He was up to his ears in alligators," North later said.

Ollie finally convinced Secord of the importance of the trip and he flew to Lisbon. In Portugal, Secord moved his stocky frame into rapid action, meeting first with the Israelis in Europe, then making a trip to Israel itself, from where he called North in Washington.

"Does Langley know of any discreet airlines that can provide the services that the Israelis were going to provide themselves?" Secord asked.

Ollie called the CIA and came back with the name of an airline, which agreed to do the job for Secord. But before it was over, it was, as North said, "a bit of a horror story."

The original plan worked out by the Israelis was to put eighty of the Hawks on a 747 cargo jet. But the only plane Secord could get had a door configuration that would allow the plane to load only eighteen Hawks. The plane took off for Tehran but North's problems with the shipment were only beginning. One of the several go-betweens, who now included Israeli arms dealers Al Schwimmer and Yaacov Nimrodi, in addition to Ghorbanifar, may have mistakenly told the Iranians that the Hawks they were receiving had the capability of shooting down high-altitude Soviet or Iraqi planes.

When the Hawks arrived in Tehran, the Iranians first became incensed by the small number delivered. Later, they disassembled one of the missiles and discovered that it was a typical Hawk—only useful against relatively low-flying aircraft. The Iranians became, in North's words, "ballistic."

North, the families of the hostages, and the Oval Office waited for word from Lebanon. When would the next hostage be released? After a few days, it became obvious that the last delivery had failed. None of the Americans came out of their Lebanon captivity.

The White House was distraught. Opinion within the inner circle, even within the NSC itself, started to turn against the Iranian Initiative. Only one hostage had been released, despite several Israeli shipments of arms to Tehran. Was the entire plan an Iranian fraud? But North felt he didn't have the luxury of believing that. His only hope was to be resolute about creating an anti-Soviet opening to Iran, praying that the hostages would be saved as a result of his efforts.

At two in the morning of December 4, 1985, with the coffee pot perking in his third floor office in the Old Executive Office Building, North sat in front of a word processor, composing a critical five page memo to Admiral Poindexter advocating that the Iranian Initiative be continued. The November foul-up had alienated both him and the Iranians. North was now presenting his argument why the United States should take direct control of the arms shipments. North was convinced the NSC could do better and that they could not afford to stop now.

"Given . . . the mistrust that the Iranians obviously feel," he wrote, "we believe that if we stop the current effort at this point and do not at least proceed with a 'test' of the current relationship, we . . . run the risk of never being able to establish a 'foothold' for the longer term goals."

He, the Israelis and the Iranians had been talking for "two nearly frantic weeks," North explained, ever since the disastrous Hawk delivery. They were getting close to agreement on the terms for the release of *all* the hostages on December 12, 1985, in exchange for a large U.S.-supported Israeli shipment of Hawks and 3300 Tows.

The deliveries would commence on December 12, in sequence, each followed by the release of another hostage.

At H-Hour a 707 would land with 300 TOWS and one American hostage would be released in Lebanon.

At H plus 10 hours, 300 more TOWS would be delivered and another American citizen released.

At H plus 16 hours, a 747 would land in Tehran and 50 Hawks and 400 TOWS would be delivered. Two American citizens would be released.

At H plus 20 hours, a 707 would discharge 300 TOWs and one American would be released.

At H plus 24 hours, a 747 would deliver 2000 TOWs and a French citizen would be released in Lebanon.

Once the hostages have been released, they would be flown to Larnaca, in Cyprus, on a Navy HH-53, where they would be picked up by a C-141 and taken to Wiesbaden, Germany, for debriefing. To put the plan into action, North explained, he would fly to London for a Saturday morning meeting with Secord and the Israelis.

He ended his note to Poindexter with a plea: "Like you and Bud, I find the idea of bartering over the lives of these poor men repugnant. Nonetheless, I believe that we are, at this point, barring unforeseen developments in London or Tel Aviv, too far along with the Iranians to risk turning back now. If we do not at least make one more try at this point, we stand a good chance of condemning some or all to death."

On December 7, 1985, the President called the first formal Cabinet meeting on the Iranian question. Reagan presented the problem and asked for comments. Secretary of State Schultz and Secretary of Defense Weinberger were negative, recommending ending the entire initiative. But Poindexter presented his, and North's case, and won the day. From then on, the arms shipments to Iran would be handled directly by the United States rather than by Israel.

On January 17, 1986, President Regan signed a "finding" authorizing the project.

North had won the internal battle, but his plan to free all the hostages on December 12 had failed. The Iranians were bargaining for larger stakes including long-term American aid and Israeli technical help in getting their meager air force modernized and flying again.

Neither North, nor the President, nor the Israelis were willing to go that far at this point, but the President wanted the initiative to continue as a sign of good faith.

During the week beginning February 17, 1986, General Secord delivered 1,000 TOWs to Iran. But still nothing was heard out of Lebanon. There were no hostage releases beyond the original one—Benjamin Weir.

That February shipment of arms to Iran was a most significant one. Not so much in its military importance, but in what it meant to Ollie North. To him, now almost desperate about the financial plight of his Contras, it was a way out— a chance to finance the resistance even if Congress refused to act. The President had given him a mandate to keep the Contras alive. He now thought he had found the key to their survival.

It was in the mathematics of the arms sale. The Pentagon had been charging the CIA $6,000 per TOW anti-tank missile in the transactions authorized by the President. In all, the President had approved the sale of 4,000 TOWs to Iran. Secord was charging the Iranians $10,000 per TOW, and North understood that Ghorbanifar had marked that up higher, perhaps to $13,000, or more.

North had not thought of the idea, but he was convinced that it was a good one. It had originated at a meeting in London. Ghorbanifar was there, and during a break in the negotiations, North and the Iranian adjourned to the bathroom. They started to talk about the difference between the prices paid for the arms by North's group and what they were charging him.

Why not, Ghorbanifar asked North, use the residual money—the spread between what they were paying for the TOWs and what they were getting—to finance the Contras?

North responded to the idea quickly. Perhaps he had found the answer to the riddle of supporting the Contras without government funds. The "residuals" per TOW amounted to $4,000 each. That, multiplied by 4,000 TOWs was $16 million. He was sure Secord would cooperate. But what would Admiral Poindexter think? North couldn't proceed on such a unique idea without the approval of his superior, and, he presumed, the President of the United States.

North quickly checked with the NSC chief, who enthusiastically endorsed the plan. North was jubilant. From the February TOW shipment by Second, North learned, over $3 million was sent to the Contras through numbered Swiss bank accounts maintained by Contra leader Adolfo Calero in Switzerland.

The upcoming May 25 trip to Tehran, on which he would accompany former NSC chief McFarlane, offered even greater opportunity. Here was a chance to met the Iranians face-to-face on their home ground. North expected he could work out the final arrangement for the release of the hostages, and the true beginnings of a diplomatic initiative. Now, there was an added inducement—the possibility of more residuals to finance the Contras.

Secord arranged the transportation for the Tehran journey by leasing two Boeing 707s. He paid $630,000 in advance and the planes took off from Kelly Air Force Base in San Antonio, Texas, loaded with Hawks and TOWs, as promised the Iranians by McFarlane and North. But the planes were not headed directly for Tehran.

Instead, the 707s landed in Tel Aviv, where the cargo was transferred to two unmarked Israeli Air Force 707s. One plane carried North and the others, along with a cargo of only one pallet of arms—about one-fifth the total. The other plane, to be held in reserve in Tel Aviv, carried the bulk of the shipment.

At the Tehran meetings, where North and McFarlane were reportedly talking with Hossein Sheikholislam—a former student leader and now deputy foreign minister—the Iranian quickly expressed his disappointment.

"We were told that one-half the equipment would be brought with McFarlane. You did not bring one-half," he complained. "This behavior raises doubts about what can be accomplished."

North explained that within "two hours" after the hostages were released and in American hands in a boat waiting off the Lebanese coast, the second 707 would land in Tehran with the rest of the TOWs and Hawks.

The meeting was rich with distrust, the Iranians arguing they must have the arms first. Immediately after, they promised, they would release the hostages. North and McFarlane stressed that they had been fooled before. It was hostages first, or no deal. For three days, they talked, generally in circles, the Iranians fearful that once the hostages were released there would be no more arms, now or ever.

North tried to reassure them that after the hostage "hurdle" had been surmounted, the United States wished to open a new diplomatic front with Iran. The two countries had many strategic goals in common: a free Afghanistan, an Iran not intimidated by the Soviet Union on its borders, and peace in Lebanon.

"There are factions in our government that don't want something like this to succeed," North told the Iranians. "McFarlane took a risk urging our president to do this. We have to be able to show progress, not for personal reasons, but for the future. This is not a deal of weapons for the release of hostages. It has to do with what we see regarding Soviet intentions in the region. We accept the Iranian revolution and respect your sovereignty. Some people want to ensure that our countries find a common foundation for the future."

By 11:30 P.M. on the night of May 27, the wrangling between the Americans and the Iranians had produced no results. The obstacle was whether it would be arms first or hostages first, an argument that could not be resolved.

Just minutes before, McFarlane had discovered that his orders to refuel the 707 were not carried out. "I think we best pack up and leave," he told North. "They're just stringing us along to see how much more they can get."

The meeting ended abruptly, but at 2:00 A.M., the Iranian delegation leader desperately called North, asking for a delay of four hours. "By 6:00 A.M. you will get your answer on the hostages," he assured him.

At 7:50, the Iranian reappeared. "We think two hostages can get out now, but it will require joint action on the other two," he told the Americans.

"It's too late," McFarlane responded. "We are leaving now."

The Iranian pleaded for the Americans to stay, that it would all work out. North wanted to remain, to take out as many hostages as they could negotiate for. But McFarlane, acting on orders from the White House, had conclusively made up his mind. It was to be all or none.

By 8:00 A.M., the American delegation was on its way to the airport. As they boarded the Israeli 707, the Iranian leader, who had followed them, asked plaintively:

"Why are you leaving?"

"Tell your superiors," McFarlane answered, "that this was the fourth time they failed to honor an agreement. The lack of trust will endure for a long time. An important opportunity was lost."

The 707 rose off the runway at 8:55 A.M. as Ollie North looked out the cabin window, distraught.

In his dismay, North could think of only one saving factor. He waited until the plane landed safely in Israel, then turned to McFarlane and offered a consoling word.

"Upon arrival . . . the other guys in my party were unloading the baggage and personal effects from the aircraft," McFarlane remembers. "I suppose I was obviously dispirited by the events in Tehran. And Colonel North, I think in an effort to be supportive, mentioned to me offhandedly that I shouldn't count it a total loss."

What Ollie North had told the surprised former NSC chief was that some of the funds from the Iranian arms sales were being diverted to the cause of the Nicaraguan rebels.

. . .

The failure of the Tehran meeting under-scored one fact: North needed a "Second Channel" of contact with the Iranian regime, perhaps someone closer to power.

He turned the job over to Secord and Hakim. In July of 1986, Secord reported back that they had found such an individual, proposed by an Iranian friend of Hakim's living in London. He was a key person, supposedly the kin to a very high official, probably Rafsanjani himself. The first meeting, held in London on July 25, 1986, between George Cave, Hakim and the "Relative," as they dubbed him, seemed quite en-couraging.

Meanwhile, the "First Channel," whose representative had been left in frustration at the Tehran Airport watching North and McFarlane return to Israel, did not wait for additional arms. Fearful that their "American Initiative" was evaporating, on July 26, 1986, the Iranians obtained the release of hostage Reverend Lawrence Jenco, who was returned safely to the States.

The Americans picked up the thread of the

Second Channel in August, again at a meeting in London. This one was attended by Secord, Hakim, the "Relative" and other Iranians. That same month they met again in Brussels, where over a period of two and a half days Secord grilled the Iranians. He then reported back to North with the information, which, in turn, North brought to the CIA for study. North concluded that they were dealing with "the real thing."

Encouraged, he now felt confident that he could move the operation forward a massive step by inviting the three Iranians from the Second Channel to Washington for meetings in September, from the 19th to the 21st.

"They were told that they would meet with direct representatives of the President," Secord explained. "And they did."

Unable to arrange a CIA plane, North turned to Secord, who smuggled the Iranians into the U.S. in a private jet that flew out of an undisclosed location in the Middle East, up through Europe, across the Northern Atlantic into Dulles Airport. CIA men met them at the airport, rushing them through Customs. From there, Secord brought the Iranians to the old Executive Office Building, where they conferred with North and Cave.

The group held several days of meetings in

North's office, both sides carefully outlining their objectives. North wanted to lay the groundwork for a future meeting, on neutral territory, for high officials of both governments, he told his guests from Tehran. The objective: a working relationship that would block Soviet encroachment in the Persian Gulf region. The Iranians discussed their urgent need for weapons and intelligence to be used in their war against Iraq, a nation, they continually stressed, that was an ally of the Soviet Union.

To continue the new relationship, both sides agreed to set up a secret eight-man Iranian-American commission. North liked the idea but warned that unless any communication to Tehran came from Cave, Secord or North, "there is no official message from the United States."

Things were progressing so well that late one night, North suggested that he give the Iranians an escorted tour of the White House. A few days later, the President was briefed on Ollie North's latest efforts, including the late night tour.

The Iranians departed, leaving North and Secord optimstic about the future of both the hostages and the diplomatic initiative. "We were well on the road to achieving the kind of contact that the United States was really looking for and truly needs," says Secord. "I believe we were on the verge of a substantial breakthrough."

North agreed. Meetings between U.S. State Department officials and their Iranian equivalents would soon materialize, he was sure.

He was pleased that he had achieved several of his goals. The funds from the Iranian arm sales were flowing to the Contras. And if he could believe the Second Channel people, which he tended to—the remaining hostages would be coming home soon.

Perhaps most important, the vital initiative to bring Iran into the anti-Soviet camp was proceeding on target. He owed it all, he was convinced, to the extraordinary secrecy that had surrounded the project. No one in Congress and only a few in the NSC and the White House were aware of the two-year-long clandestine effort.

If that confidence could be kept a while longer, Ollie North believed that he would add a geopolitical victory to his White House dossier that was greater and more rewarding than any he had accomplished before.

*Nine*

---

# The Unraveling

IT SOMETIMES AMAZED, AND ALWAYS PLEASED, Oliver North that despite his complex, worldwide covert enterprise on behalf of the President, his network was still a secret.

For an affable, gregarious man who didn't seem the type to husband a secret, he maintained the security of his Contra supply network and Iranian arms sales—then the marriage of the two in the diversion of funds—with extraordinary success.

Almost singlehandedly, he kept the three operations going with little major help, other than that from General Secord. The continuation of the Iranian arms negotiations, which by the summer of 1986 had provided freedom for two hostages, was mainly the result of North's perserverance.

One CIA division chief described him during this period as a "man with a lot of energy and a lot of determination who essentially kept it alive because of the President's personal and emotional interest in getting the hostages out."

For over a year and a half, North had been keeping an extraordinarily low profile on the Iranian project, divulging it to no one on the outside, holding the secret of his meetings and trips to Europe within a tight circle that included Fawn Hall, McFarlane, Poindexter, and very few of the one hundred-and-fifty staffers at the National Security Council. The diversion, of course, was known to no one except Poindexter, then McFarlane.

The same was true of the Contra resupply operation. C-123 flights flew regularly out of Ilapango in El Salvador and Aguacate in eastern Honduras and dropped a massive amount of supplies by parachute into Nicaragua. In four months of that year, North coordinated at least nine arms shipments to the Contras. Yet nothing had thus far appeared in the media.

But there was one activity that Colonel North could hardly hide—his open efforts on behalf of the Contra fund-raising. His slide presentations were legend in the Washington Beltway and he was becoming the bete noire of the Democratic Party left, most of whom opposed arming the Nicaraguan rebels.

Congress was getting suspicious that this energetic young Marine on the President's staff was doing more than making speeches. "Be cautious," Poindexter warned North.

The first stirring that Congress was taking an interest in the activities of the many-hatted North came on March 10, 1986, in a note from his former boss, Bud McFarlane, who had left the NSC in 1985 but was still working for the President as a consultant.

"I would expect the heat from the Hill to become immense on you by summer," McFarlane warned.

That didn't surprise North, but what followed did.

"Consequently, it strikes me as wise that you leave the White House."

North didn't take the suggestion seriously. There were three more hostages to get out, and the Contra movement was far from secure. Congress had not yet voted them a penny for fiscal '86–'87. Besides, McFarlane admitted, he was giving "a knee jerk reaction" to the coming Contra furor in Congress. But he also took space to praise North's virtual indispensability:

"At the same time, there will be no one to do all (or even a small part of what) you have done. And if it isn't done, virtually all the investment of the past five years will go down the drain."

McFarlane then offered a scenario for the future:

"1. North leaves the White House in May (1986) and takes 30 days leave. 2. July 1st North is assigned as a fellow at the CSIS [Center for Strategic and International Studies at Georgetown University where McFarlane had gone as a fellow] and (lo and behold) is assigned to McFarlane's office. 3. McFarlane/North continue to work the Iran account as well as to build other clandestine capabilities so much in demand here and there."

North didn't quit. But he sensed that there were people on his trail, mainly those in Congress who opposed the Contras and correctly suspected that he had been acting as the White House's clandestine agent in Central America.

In May of 1986, North sent a note to Poindexter outlining his fears:

"The more money there is (and we will have a considerable amount in a few more days) the more visible the program becomes (airplanes, pilots, weapons, deliveries, etc.) and the more inquisitive will become people like [U.S. Representatives] Kerry, Barnes, Harkins, et al.

While I care not a whit what they say about me, it could well be a political embarrassment for the President and you."

McFarlane agreed, relaying his concern to Poindexter. Again he argued that it might be time for Ollie North to move on, to retire from the complex network of intrigue, to get out before everything blew up in his, and the President's, face.

"The Democratic left is coming after him with a vengeance," McFarlane warned, and "eventually they will get him."

McFarlane proved ominously correct but the lieutenant colonel still had some maneuvering room left.

On June 24, 1986, the White House received a request that North appear before the House Permanent Select Committee on Intelligence to explain his actions on behalf of the Contras. It took a vote in Congress to bring the reluctant warrior up Pennsylvania Avenue. House Resulution 485 was introduced, directing the President of the United States to provide the House of Representatives with:

"Certain information concerning activities of Lieutenant Colonel North or any other member of the staff of the National Security Council in support of the resistance."

Instead, later that summer, the President provided Oliver North himself. From the White House's point of view, North was much better than any possibly incriminating documents.

North thought carefully about what he would tell them. He didn't believe he was breaking the Boland Amendment, but unlike combat in Vietnam, discretion in Washington politics was usually more productive than valor. Surely, Congress was no one to confide in on this issue.

The truth, he was afraid, would destroy the Contra movement, eventually leaving the Communists in full control of Central America barring, of course, a major war that would involve Cuba and perhaps even the Soviet Union. Neither was he willing to destroy his years of work in developing a resistance to the Sandinistas.

Ollie unflinchingly dissembled. He told the congressmen that he knew of no specific military operation by the Nicaraguan resistance. He had given no military advice or assistance to the Contras.

"Well done," Poindexter complimented North. The admiral was relieved that knowledge of the covert Contra operation was secure, at least for the time being.

The first signs of outside security breaches were also beginning to appear.

Poindexter had heard from another NSC staffer that North had offered to loan the CIA a

Danish-registered ship. The Vice Admiral was less concerned about the bravado of the offer than the fact that news of the gesture had leaked back to the NSC.

"I'm afraid you're letting your operational role become too public," Poindexter admonished North. "From now on, I don't want you to talk to anybody else, including Casey, except me about any of your operational roles."

The advice was well taken, especially since North did not feel that the CIA was sufficiently secure. In a peculiar twist of events, the field grade officer had become a one-man CIA of staggering proportions.

North's performance before the Congress had stilled some of the worries, but not all. As the summer of 1986 progressed, there were more insidious leaks, more questions from the Hill. They were only rumors; there was no hard evidence tying Ollie to anything. Still his name, or oblique references to him, kept turning up in print. In one case, at least, it went beyond the Contra project and touched on the super-secret Iranian arms sale.

On June 29, 1986, a Jack Anderson and Dale Van Atta column in the *Washington Post* stated flatly: "We can reveal that the secret negotiations over arms supply and release of American hostages have involved members of the National Security Council and a former official of the CIA."

The once-unknown Marine was slowly becoming a controversial person in the Beltway area, even gaining a group of "Ollie haters." They leaked stories to the press that his tour at the NSC had come to an end. Poindexter, they said, was graciously trying to ease him out without alienating the President.

Since North had become the darling of the Contra lecture circuit, the rumors only created more press as conservatives rallied to save one of the staunchest guardians of the Reagan Doctrine. Columnists Rowland Evans and Robert Novak, anticipating that his enemies would get the leatherneck's hide, were already lamenting his loss. It was, they said, "a symbol of the degradation of the once-mighty NSC staff."

The Marine was flattered, and embarrassed, by the attention. Finally, he decided to offer his resignation to Admiral Poindexter.

If the rumors were true, it would be accepted.

"I can understand why you may well have reservations about both my involvement in Nicaragua policy and even my continued tenure here," he wrote the admiral. "It probably would be best if I were to move on quietly, but expeditiously as possible. I want you to know that it is, for me, deeply disappointing to have lost your confidence . . . You should not be expected to retain on your staff someone who could be talking to the media or whom you believe to be too emotionally involved in an issue to be objective in the development of policy options and recommendations. I know in my heart that this is not the case, but as I said in our discussion yesterday, we live in a world of perceptions, not realities."

The cool, studied Poindexter, himself a nuclear physicist, issued a simple reply. "Now you are getting emotional again."

That was that. Ollie North stayed on, having again outflanked his enemies.

He had won in more ways than one. On June 25, by a vote of 221 to 209, the House had made an abrupt about-face on the Contras. Instead of prohibiting all government aid for the rebels, as they had for two years, they now voted $100 million for the fiscal year beginning October 1. The money was to be administered by the CIA, the same group that had once been prohibited from helping the Contras—forcing North, Secord, et al. to become the substitute CIA.

North was jubilant, but he was still worried about two things: he had to keep the operation going until October, then accomplish a smooth transition.

"We are rapidly approaching the point where Project Democracy assets in CentAm need to be turned over to CIA for use in new program," he wrote Poindexter. The assets were considerable: six aircraft, warehouses, supplies, maintenance facilities, ships, boats, leased houses, vehicles, communications equipment and the secret Costa Rica airstrip. The value, conservatively, was $4.5 million.

Ollie North's clandestine empire was in place, and ready to be transferred over to the government that had once scorned it.

Meanwhile, the Iranian Initiative was in full gear. North had new hope that the Second Channel would produce the release of the last three hostages.

Earlier, a frustrated McFarlane had advocated a strike force assault on terrorist locations in Beirut to free the Americans. North had counseled moderation. Now he was pleased that the chance for release of the three looked promising—if secrecy could be continued. Articles such as Jack Anderson's frightened North, but the press in general seemed not to suspect anything.

He was optimistic, but still realistic. Ollie knew that the very concept of arms-for-hostages had placed the United States in an unenviable—if unavoidable—position.

"It is entirely possible," North wrote, "that if nothing is received (the Iranian official) will be killed by his opponents in Tehran, Ghorbanifar will be killed by his creditors (they are the beneficiaries of a $22 million insurance policy), and one American hostage will probably be killed in order to demonstrate their displeasure."

On Sunday, October 5, 1986, a worn Ollie North left Washington, D.C., as "William P. Goode" and boarded a military aircraft headed for Frankfurt, Germany. He was on his way to meet the Iranians once more, hoping the Second Channel would perform as expected.

He had brought an unusual gift with him from President Reagan. After the "Relative," the contact from the Second Channel, revealed he was bringing a Koran for the President, North—as a "reciprocal gesture"—brought a Bible. North thought it would enhance the gift if the President cited a passage in front of the volume. He had already found the appropriate passage, Galatians, chapter 3, verse 8:

And the Scripture, forseeing that God would justify the Gentiles by faith, preached the gospel beforehand to Abraham, saying, 'All the nations shall be blessed in you.'

The verse was important, he told Poindexter. It was a New Testament reference to Abraham, who is revered by Jews, Christians and Moslems.

As usual, North had done his homework, providing the detail that earned him kudos from some for his "sensitivity," and brickbats from his enemies for his skill at "manipulation."

In any case, it was a demonstration of his bravado. "It would be most effective," he told Poindexter, "if the President handwrote the inscription and initialed/signed it without addressing the note to any particular person."

Poindexter delivered the Bible to the President, who did just as his favorite Marine asked.

Armed with the Bible, North headed for the meeting in Mainz, Germany, in an optimistic mood. He had arranged the groundrules for this confab, which was to be the final one on the hostages. No written documents would be left with the Iranians. All communications between "Tango" (Tehran) and the U.S. team would be verbal.

The meeting opened on a bright note. The "Relative" assured North that he would soon have good news about the "obstacles" (hostages) to better Iranian-American relations. North assured them of American good faith, which would soon be backed by more arms.

North presented the Bible to the "Relative," ostensibly kin to Rafsanjani. In his earnest voice, North launched into a pious recital for the fundamentalist Iranians.

"We had an enormous debate, a very angry debate, inside our government over whether my President should authorize me to say, 'We accept the Islamic Revolution of Iran as a fact,' " North began, his voice rising like that of a television evangelist. "The President went off one whole weekend and prayed about what the answer should be . . . with that passage that he wrote in the front of the Bible. And he said to me, 'This is a promise that God gave to Abraham. Who am I to say that we should not do this?' "

Impressed, the Iranians gave North the Koran for the President, then offered a gift for himself, a Persian rug of considerable value. Politely, North turned it down.

North treated the meeting as if it were his last chance to negotiate for the hostages. His political imagination took off in full flight. He told them he had met with President Reagan in Camp David, and that the chief executive wished them an "honorable victory." Their opponent, Iraq's leader Saddam Husain, "must go."

It was a show, "my donkey act," as North said.

"I'd have told them they could have free tickets to Disneyworld or a trip on the space shuttle if it would have gotten the Americans home."

Over the next two days, North and Secord hammered out a seven-point plan with the Iranians. In return for the delivery of 500 TOW missiles, they would arrange the release of two of the three hostages still under Hezbollah control.

Ollie North felt vindicated. His insistence on continuing the Iranian connection was paying off.

．　．　．

While North, imbued with high hopes, was parlaying with the Iranians, his world was crumbling outside. Not slowly, but with the swift impact of a Soviet SAM missile striking one of the Contra resupply C-123K cargo planes over the jungles of Nicaragua.

In the Old Executive Office Building, Lieutenant Colonel Robert Earl, North's aide, received word of the crash from Honduras and immediately sent Poindexter a computer message. "It is overdue from its mission and no radio contact was received. It is currently unknown where or why the aircraft went down, but (third country) assets are discreetly organizing a SAR

(Search and Rescue) effort. "The last words were ominous: "Three Americans and one Nicaraguan national aboard."

Even though the two year proscription on aid to the Contras had officially ended on October 1, and the American government and the Contras were now allied, the downed cargo plane became a public relations nightmare for the administration—and its chief Contra protagonist Ollie North.

Eugene Hasenfus, a former CIA cargo handler, was the only survivor and he was talking, telling the world it was all "U.S. government controlled." The Sandinistas were screaming, but they were pleased, vowing to place Hasenfus on trial as an example of *Yanqui* intervention.

A White House aide futilely tried to project a positive view of the incident. "If it had happened before the ban, we would be up the creek."

North, a sophisticated observer, knew that he was in immediate need of a paddle, a large one. Hasenfus was an employee of the Contra resupply effort organized by Secord and himself.

"We urgently need to find a high-powered lawyer and benefactor who can raise a legal defense for Hasenfus in Managua," North told McFarlane on October 12. "If we can find such persons we can not only hold Gene and Sally Hasenfus together (i.e., on our side, not pawns of the Sandinista propaganda machine) but can make some significant headway of our own in counterattacking the media."

North added that he was sending a Swiss lawyer to Managua, instructing him to cooperate fully with the high-powered attorney, "whoever he is." North had already lined up someone to donate $100,000 to the defense fund.

As journalists tried to connect Hasenfus to the CIA, the covert actions North had protected for so long started to unravel—even the well-guarded Iranian connection. Roy Furmark, a New York energy consultant and longtime friend of William Casey, told the CIA director that a group of Canadian businessmen he knew were threatening to expose the Iran arms deal, claiming they had not recovered money they had invested. Casey asked CIA-man Charles Allen, a member of North's Frankfurt negotiating team, to check it out.

"I could see this thing blowing up," said Allen. "We were going to have an incredible mess on our hands," Allen said.

The unraveling scenario was disturbing to North, but he tried to keep his sights on the next connection: an October 26 meeting in Frankfurt with their Second Channel intermediaries.

That conference could bring home two more hostages and distract attention from the Hasenfus debacle.

But when North arrived in Germany, the Iranians immediately reported a change in the arrangements. Try as they would, they could arrange the release of only one American held by the Hezbollah. After all, they insisted, *they* were not holding the hostages. Would North prefer to wait until two hostages were available and move them out together?

North immediately communicated with the White House. "The decision was taken by Poindexter in Washington," Secord recounts, "to go ahead and get the one and proceed on with the job, and then get to the high-level mission."

Before leaving Frankfurt, the Iranians imparted some more bad news. The entire Iranian Initiative was coming unglued. The hard-line faction headed by Khomeini's appointed successor, Ayatollah Montazeri, had learned of North's trip to Tehran the previous May and was going to expose the story. In fact, Secord recalled them saying that "five million leaflets were being printed at the University of Tehran at the time," revealing the details of the American connection.

The news made the hostage release that much more urgent, North believed. It was too late for the President to reconsider. Once the operation was exposed, the gate would be closed on the hostages' freedom. President Reagan gave the order for the shipment and Secord arranged for 500 TOWs to leave for Tehran.

North flew to Cyprus, still hopeful that two, rather than one, hostage would come out. An uncharacteristic note to Poindexter describes his mood, an extreme indication of frustration after years of effort.

"This is the damnedest operation I have ever seen. Please let me go onto other things," North pleaded. "Would like very much to give RR two hostages that he can take credit for and stop worrying about these other things."

On October 31, "Mr. Goode" and General Secord secretly entered Lebanon, exposing themselves to the same fate as those they were working to free. Meeting with American Ambassador John Kelly, they told him of the need for greater precautions. The impending release of the next hostage might be accompanied by exposure of the project and unexpected local trouble. He had to be careful. Three hours after they entered Lebanon, North and Secord were on their way.

On Cyprus, North waited. Finally, in the early

morning hours of November 2, Ambassador Kelly received a call instructing him to proceed to the embassy's old west annex. There he found a bearded and worn David Jacobsen, a free man after seventeen months of captivity. On his person was a message that was quickly broadcast worldwide.

"Proceed with current approaches that could lead, if continued, to a solution of the hostage issue," the cryptic note said.

As the world wondered what the kidnapper's message meant, Ollie North watched the unfolding events with a sense of fatalism. His days as NSC quarterback were now numbered. He only hoped he had enough time before the full exposure to gain the freedom of the last two Americans, Terry Anderson and Thomas Sutherland.

But it was not to be.

While North was still on Cyprus, he was informed by Washington that a Lebanese weekly, *Al Shiraa* (Sailboat Mast), had published the story he had always feared would one day be revealed. Though riddled with factual errors, the article in the small magazine had correctly reported the main elements of the story—of his and McFarlane's trip to Tehran to obtain the release of the hostages, and provide Iran with much needed arms.

Within hours the news spread throughout the world. Ollie North knew that his extraordinary days as a clandestine ambassador for the President of the United States were over.

*Ten*

---

# Keeping the Lid On

OVERNIGHT, OLIVER NORTH HAD BECOME A man virtually without a country.

He had lost control over events in Nicaragua and Iran, and his White House power was elusively slipping away. Once his role was exposed, the strong ties between himself and the Presidency were strained, and would probably soon be cut. The loyal soldier had always known that he would eventually have to offer up, if not his life, at least his reputation, for his country. That time was drawing inescapably near.

The Iran arms affair was rapidly escalating into a national scandal that threatened to undermine the Presidency. What did Ronald

Reagan know and when did he know it? The question was whispered at first, then shouted. It was broadcast throughout the land, a Nixonian *redux*, the reaper of contemporary history thrusting Watergate upon the nation—again.

But was this really a Watergate? People tried "Irangate," but those who understood knew that this was really Ollie North's show, his triumph and defeat, the tragedy of his unhestitating service to his President, to his commander in chief.

As the stories broke around him, Oliver North stayed in Cyprus, conferring constantly with Ambassador John Kelly, *still* hoping that Terry Anderson or Thomas Sutherland would be released.

North, who sometimes boasted that someday he would have to fall on his Marine sword for his country, seemed relaxed. He kept his usual schedule, fielding calls from worried contacts around the world. The day after he returned from his fruitless Cyprus vigil, he attended a banquet in honor of Contra fundraiser Carl Channell.

The following day, November 8, as if there had been no operational debacle, North journeyed back to Europe for still one more try at hostage negotiations with his Iranian intermediaries. The ensuing three-day Geneva talks covered a wide range of topics, including a possible exchange of Dawa prisoners being held in Kuwait. But the talks foundered, made important by the publicity in the United States.

North returned home, seemingly calm as events whirled around him. No one could say the same for the rest of the Reagan Administration.

. . .

At the National Security Council, damage control was in effect. Poindexter called McFarlane and asked him to maintain silence.

"We have to keep the lid on," the National Security Advisor somberly told his former chief.

Between them, Poindexter and McFarlane knew more about the covert operations than anyone except North himself. Poindexter, North's superior, parlayed with other NSC people and, against the advice of some, including McFarlane, chose not to talk.

On the same day that *Al Shiraa* printed the news, Secretary of State George Shultz sent a cable to Poindexter. The best course of action, he said, was to make it "clear that this was a special one-time operation based on humanitarian grounds and decided by the President within his Constitutional responsibility to act in the service of the national interest."

But Poindexter rejected that advice. Public statements, he insisted, would jeopardize the lives of the hostages. He also wanted time to prepare before his staff people testified in front of the congressional intelligence committees. The admiral told Shultz that he believed in the necessity of being "absolutely close-mouthed, while stressing that the basic policy toward Iran, the Gulf War and dealing with terrorists had not changed."

Many in the administration were surprised by the fast-breaking story. Some, like Secretary Shultz, did not even know about the January 17 Finding in which President Reagan first authorized direct arms shipments to Iran.

At the White House, the enormous emotional energy that the President had put into North's attempt to free the hostages had not yet dissipated. Despite the bad news, the President still hoped to get them all out of Lebanon. Secrecy seemed the most effective route. News of McFarlane's trip to Iran, he told the press later that day, had "no foundation." Buying time, the President also denied any kind of arms-for-hostages deal with the Iranians.

"May I suggest and appeal to you with regard to this," the President asked an unresponsive news media, "that the speculation, the commenting on a story that came out of the Middle East and that to us, has no foundation—all of that is making it more difficult to get the other hostages out."

The truth had been sacrificed to Reagan's increasingly obsessive worry about the lives of the victims. The hostages had the most to loose, of course. No one appreciated that more than just-released David Jacobsen. At a welcoming ceremony at the White House, Jacobsen went the President one step further by making an emotional appeal to the press.

"Unreasonable speculation on your part can endanger their lives," he warned. When the reporters aggressively followed him, the President and the First Lady up the steps into the White House, still shouting questions about the Iran arms deal, Jacobsen, his face reddened in anger, turned.

"In the name of God, would you please be responsible and back off" he cried.

The essence of power in the hostage-taking act is bluff. Now that the game was exposed— the sleight-of-hand revealed—was there anything left to barter with?

In September, Louis Boccardi, President of the Associated Press, had visited Oliver North seeking information on his Beirut correspondent Terry Anderson, who had been held by the Hezbollah since March 16, 1985.

"I sure hope you are dealing with someone regarding Terry and the others in Lebanon," Boccardi told North, "and that you can keep it quiet. That's the only way any of this will work."

Reagan and staff were trying to follow that advice to keep things quiet. But in a democracy, particulary one addicted to an unending supply of gossip and news, there was no stopping the press, nor the Congress, nor the millions of Americans waiting for the answers to two questions:

Why did America sell arms to a terrorist-sponsor nation? Why did America trade arms for hostages?

Ollie North had his own answers, but he was not talking.

．　．　．

In Tehran, Ali Akbar Rafsanjani, whose "Relative" North had been negotiating with, called a press conference himself. His aim: to denounce the Americans with whom he had been dealing. The turbaned Speaker of the Iranian *Majlis,* or parliament, claimed that Robert McFarlane and four other Americans had come to Tehran secretly and illegally—uninvited—but were detained at the airport before being sent away.

A week later, Iranian Prime Minister Mousavi again decried the United States as the "Great Satan," refusing to help release any hostages as long as the U.S. continued to hold up delivery of arms purchased before the Shah fell in 1979.

It was becoming increasingly difficult to keep the lid on.

Reports of American arms deals were coming in from all over the world. A Rome newspaper reported that "5,000 tons of spares for F-104s" were shipped from Italy on behalf of the American government. A French wire service said that a large shipment of arms left Portugal bound for Iran aboard a Panamian-registered freighter.

As the news stories, many exaggerated, circulated around Washington, Poindexter realized he would have to consider preparations for going public. At lunch with McFarlane, Poindexter said: "We've got to put together a full chronology."

"Get it all out," McFarlane encouraged.

Normally the most tight-lipped of the White House staff, rivaled in secret-keeping only by the President himself, Poindexter inadvertently revealed a key piece of information to the press.

To a group of journalists assembled for a "back-grounder" on the affair, Poindexter stated:

"There are other countries involved."

"This shipment to Israel?" one journalist fished.

"I'm not confirming that."

"Was it in our behalf?" the reporter pressed.

The professional clandestine manager stumbled.

"It was done in our interest," he responded, then quieted.

Another piece of the puzzle had fallen into place. Poindexter had admitted that the Israelis were involved in the Iranian connection. It had added to the sinister allure of the affair. Israel was as much Iran's enemy as was America. If America was the "Great Satan," Israel was surely the "Little Satan," as victimized by terrorism as was the United States.

Why then, the press wanted to know, were both countries selling arms to Iran? Did Israel pull the United States into the deal? Or was the U.S. simply using Israel as its Middle Eastern surrogate?

. . .

From Oliver North's perspective, all this was of great interest. But one special fact intrigued him. It was the relative absence of talk about the Contras, who had taken so much of his own work and emotional energy.

In Nicaragua, the "high-powered" lawyer North had requested had appeared. He was Griffin Bell, Attorney General of the United States during the Carter Administration. Sally Hasenfus had chosen him from a panel of three whose names she was given by the office of Elliott Abrams, Assistant Secretary of State for Inter-American Affairs.

The other two recommended attorneys were former Secretary of State Cyrus Vance and former Vice President Walter Mondale. Bell offered his services without charge, but Hasenfus was convicted and sentenced to thirty years, a term later commuted.

On Capitol Hill, what was to become a mammoth industry of inquiries was gearing up. The Senate Select Committee on Intelligence was already on the track of "Iranscam," one of the first—if ephemeral—labels for the affair.

A witness from the CIA, the agency's Inspector General, was among the first to talk.

Considering the aid that agency had given his own covert network, North anticipated silence.

Instead the CIA IG told the committee everything he had learned about the Contra operation. North was shocked. He was gaining an education in the reverse side of clandestine activity in America. What was once secret must be made public, with the same expenditure of energy.

Now Ollie North understood why only a week before his friend and mentor, CIA Director Bill Casey, had taken him aside and strongly advised that he hire an attorney.

. . .

The oval conference table in North's office suite was strewn with paper, scissors and scotch tape as it had been for most of the week. Outside it was already dark, and the street lights on Pennsylvania Avenue glistened in the fall chill.

It was Tuesday evening, November 18, 1986, and North and his NSC colleagues were working on the latest version of an Iran arms affair "chronology." Only days after the *Al Shiraa* revelation, Admiral Poindexter had told North to put the story together. The colonel was joined at various times by his aides, and even McFarlane.

The process was agonizing. Between November 5 and November 20, the group produced a dozen versions of what happened. President Reagan had promised the nation a press conference on November 19, the first one since the

Iran affair became public. And now Oliver North, working with his colleagues, was scrambling to find a history of events the president could support.

Poindexter had gone home for the evening, but had left word to call him if needed.

Instead, North phoned McFarlane. "We need your help on the chronology," North told his former boss. "The White House needs it to debrief the President for the press conference, and we're under the gun to get it done."

McFarlane, a Reagan loyalist in or out of office, cancelled a dinner appointment and drove to the Old Executive Office Building. He arrived at 8:00 that evening in what he described as a "feverish climate."

McFarlane was given a chair, keyboard and console and he went to work, writing his own account of events. By 10:00 P.M. he had finished his version and had skimmed a copy of the "master" chronology. McFarlane was shocked. There were a half dozen errors. The chronology, McFarlane later admitted, "was not a full and completely accurate account" of events.

The primary objective of that written account, McFarlane believed, "was to describe a sequence of events that would distance the President from the initial approval of the Iran arms sale."

Two evenings later, on Thursday at 7:30, the shredder bin in Room 302 was full. Fawn Hall and Oliver North had been culling the files for sensitive material, including the names and numbers of contacts accumulated in the course of putting together his Contra supply network, and of those who had helped him track the Second Channel.

"The more people you know, the more contacts you have in the Press or Pentagon or other government agency, the better a job you can do as an NSC officer," says Roger Fontaine, a former North collegue at the NSC.

North had done an excellent job in that area, and his files were solid evidence of the fact. But today was a day for shredding. "A shredding party," he would later quip to Bud McFarlane. An old pro at covert operations, McFarlane was hardly surprised that Ollie would be "trying to fix his files."

．　．　．

In Beltway parlance, Attorney General Ed Meese had been "tasked" by the President with learning what he could about the Iran affair. He had already started with McFarlane. The Attorney General called the former National Security Adviser at home Friday afternoon, explaining that the President had asked him to put together an accurate record of events. "I would like to talk to you," he told McFarlane, who once again dropped everything and drove to the District.

After a half hour of discussion in Meese's inner office, the Attorney General rose to close the meeting.

"Ed, the President was four-square behind this," McFarlane said. "He never had any reservations about approving anything that the Israelis wanted to do here."

McFarlane felt pressured to reveal the truth, but he also sensed the need to exercise care and preserve the Iranian connection.

Oliver North was being equally careful as he fed the documents into the shredding machine near the security safes. He spent the following evening, Friday, and much of the pre-Thanksgiving weekend culling his file folders, his steno pad diaries, memoranda and cable messages, before dispatching them to the shredder. Five-and-a-half years of work were reduced to confetti.

Determined not to "compromise the national security of the United States . . . put lives at risk . . . demonstrate a covert action," North also instructed his secretary, Fawn Hall, to alter certain documents.

In one memorandum, dated February 6, 1985, North suggested "seizing or sinking" the Nicaraguan merchant ship *Monimbo,* then bound for the port of Corinto with arms and ammunitions for the Sandinistas. The sanitized version of the document was absent his recommendation as well as Poindexter's scribbled comment: "We need to take action to make sure ship does not arrive in Nicaragua."

On Saturday morning, November 22, Lieutenant Colonel North left his Great Falls, Virginia, suburban home and opened his office in the Old Executive Office Building. Two Assistant United States Attorney Generals, Charles Cooper and Bradford Reynolds, had been dispatched by Attorney General Meese to interview North. Providing the attorneys with the documents they required, North continued his weekend-long activity. While the attorneys read, North shredded.

"I was sitting at my desk," North recalled. "They were working ten feet from me. . . . They were working on their projects; I was working on mine."

North felt secure during that informal inquiry, confident that every sensitive document that could tie the National Security Council to the Contra diversion had been destroyed during the past week.

But he was wrong.

At some point during the morning, Bradford Reynolds walked to the security safes. In one of them, he found an undated, unsigned TOP SE-CRET–SENSITIVE memo, from North to Poindexter, titled "Release of American Hostages in Beirut."

The memo detailed certain arms transfers to the Iranians, information of little value at this stage of the investigation. Reynolds read quickly through the five-page memo. At the very top of the last page Reynolds noticed it.

"The residual funds from this transaction are allocated as follows," it read. "$12 million will be used to purchase critically needed supplies for the Nicaraguan Democratic Resistance Forces."

Without betraying his find, Reynolds left the office to meet Meese for lunch. He handed the explosive document to the Attorney General, who immediately registered surprise. Reynolds had stumbled on what was to be the core of the controversy—the use of Khomeini's funds to support the Nicaraguan Contras.

Ollie North's failure to shred one vital document was to be his most costly error. "It was, for me," North later said, "the deepest, darkest secret of the whole activity."

The following day, Sunday, November 23,

North attended church, spent some time with his family and then went to Robert McFarlane's office for a 12:30 meeting. North had spent a difficult twenty-four hours weighing whether or not to divulge the full story to Meese. Without any knowledge that Meese had the sensitive memo in his possession, North told his former boss: "I'm going to have to tell the Justice Department about the diversion of funds to the Contras."

At 2:00 P.M., North headed for the Justice Department Building a few blocks away. At 2:13 the meeting began with North, Meese, Reynolds, Cooper and Richardson.

North was questioned at some length about the Iranian arms sales before Meese brought up the subject of the Contras. The Attorney General brought out the five-page memo and handed it to North, who immediately recognized the document.

"He was surprised and visibly shaken," Meese remembered.

.   .   .

Before dawn, at 0450 hours, on Monday morning, security at the Old Executive Office Building noticed that the alarm in Colonel North's office had gone off. Investigating, they found Oliver North, as usual, at his desk working.

Later that morning, Meese met with President Reagan and Chief of Staff Donald Regan to inform them about the existence of the damaging diversion memo. Before accepting it as valid, Meese suggested confirming it with others.

Regan went immediately to Admiral Poindexter and asked if he knew of North's role in a diversion. "I had a feeling that something bad was going on," Poindexter said, "but I didn't investigate and I didn't do a thing about it. I really didn't want to know. I was so damned mad at Tip O'Neill for the way he was dragging the Contras around I didn't want to know what, if anything, was going on. I should have, but I didn't."

The crucial weekend of investigation had created its own momentum. On Tuesday, at noon, Meese and the President presided at a hastily convened nationally televised press conference in the White House.

The President stunned the nation with the news of the diversion. He had ordered a full Justice Department inquiry and was inviting congressional investigation as well. His National Security Adviser, John Poindexter, would be leaving the White House and reassigned to naval duty. Colonel North was being immediately relieved of his duties on the NSC staff.

Attorney General Meese, who followed Reagan to the lecturn, explained that North "was the only person in the United States government who knew, precisely, about the diversion."

In response to a reporter's question about possible prosecution of Colonel North, Meese replied: "We are presently looking into the legal aspects of it as to whether there is any criminality involved."

Within the space of three days, Colonel North had moved from the position of a prominent White House aide with the full confidence of the President to that of a suspected felon.

That afternoon, President Reagan called the Marine and thanked him for his service to the nation. By the end of the day, the combination locks on Lieutenant Colonel North's office, Room 302, were changed.

Ollie North had ended his service.

*Eleven*

---

# The Defiant Patriot

IN A 1983 QUESTIONNAIRE MAILED TO THE graduates of the United States Naval Academy's class of 1968, the *Baltimore Sun* asked whether they were "professionally satisfied." Oliver North was, in 1983, a member of the staff of the National Security Council, an elite agency in the Executive Office of the President of the United States. His office at the corner of 17th Street and Pennsylvania Avenue, next door to the White House, was a center of American power.

"Yes," Oliver North wrote in 1983, responding to the *Sun*'s question, "though would much prefer to lead Marines in harm's way than push paper in a bureaucratic fray."

Two days after his dismissal from the NSC in November of 1986, North returned to the old ornate building next to the White House. It was Thanksgiving Day and all was quiet. He wanted to gather up a few items he had left behind, perhaps make a last tour around the rooms that had been so much a part of his life. The suddenness of his departure, his precipitous fall from favor, were reminders of how fragile were the trappings of power. His fictional "Dr. North, from the White House," was not so much a quip as a warning.

When North arrived at the ground-floor entrance to the building that Thanksgiving Day, the security guards turned him away. They were sorry, but he was no longer a staff member of the National Security Council.

Three issues dominated the nation's debate for the next eight months. Who was responsible for selling arms to Iran? Who authorized the *sub rosa* military assistance to the Contras? Did anyone besides Oliver North—the President, for instance—know about the diversion of funds from the Iran arms sale to the Nicaraguan resistance?

For most of those eight months, the one person best able to answer those questions—Oliver North—was a phantom. He withdrew from public view. He refused to talk to the press. He invoked his Fifth Amendment right against self-incrimination when asked to testify before Congress. His was an enigmatic, smiling and silent face.

That in part explains his transformation—from phantom to hero. For those eight long months he was an invisible symbol of the country's latest political identity crisis. When he appeared last July, in the Senate Caucus Room, in his olive summer dress A uniform, tall, smiling, relaxed, confident, he ended the wearying period of speculation.

On August 12, 1987, President Reagan gave a speech he hoped would place the Iran-Contra affair behind him. In a soothing, upbeat address that recognized the scandal's seriousness, the President accepted responsibility for the policy that Oliver North had been implementing. "If there is to be blame, it properly rests here in this office and with this President."

It wasn't an exoneration of Oliver North. It was a recognition of the realities of the American political system, realities of which Oliver North was fully aware.

The lieutenant colonel had not fought bravely in an unpopular war without learning the lessons of a demanding democracy. Despite the months of pressure by the press, the pollsters and the Congress, he remained resolute.

Despite being fired by his President, he remained loyal to the White House.

Reagan seemed to reciprocate. "Colonel North and Admiral Poindexter believed they were doing what I would've wanted done—keeping the democratic resistance alive in Nicaragua. I believed then and I believe now in preventing the Soviets from establishing a beachhead in Central America."

So did Oliver Laurence North.

He was loyal despite the many pressures. In the end the American people seemed to appreciate that quality above all else. After years of witnessing the tortured second-guessing of American leaders about foreign policy, North was someone who offered a positive view of America's stance. Right or wrong, in any era Ollie North would have been a patriot.

In these difficult times, he had become a defiant one.

*Appendix I*

# Citations

The President of the United States takes pleasure in presenting the BRONZE STAR MEDAL TO

SECOND LIEUTENANT
OLIVER L. NORTH
UNITED STATES MARINE CORPS

for service set forth in the following

*CITATION:*

"For heroic achievement in connection with combat operations against the enemy in the Republic of Vietnam while serving as a Platoon Commander with Company K, Third Battalion, Third Marines, Third Marine Division. On 22 February 1969, Second Lieutenant North was aboard the lead tank directing his platoon's reconnaissance operations in the vicinity of Con Thien in Quang Tri Province when his patrol came under intense automatic weapons and machine gun fire and hand grenade attack from a numerically superior North Vietnamese Army force well entrenched in the densely wooded area. Reacting instantly, he began delivering a heavy volume of return fire while directing his men and the vehicles out of the hazardous area and into open terrain. Rapidly assessing the situation, when he observed the enemy attempting to envelope and isolate his patrol, Second Lieutenant North completely disregarded his own safety as he boldly remained in his dangerously exposed position on top of the tank to deploy his men and establish a defensive perimeter. When struck by the vehicle's revolving turret and thrown to the ground, he resolutely refused medical attention and ignored his own painful injuries as he skillfully directed the actions of the Marines. Realizing that radio communication was imperative, Second Lieutenant North fearlessly moved across the fire-swept terrain, climbed aboard the tank, and remained oblivious to the North Vietnamese rounds impacting around him as he retrieved the radio from atop the tank and directed his radio operator to establish contact with supporting aircraft. Obtaining an M-79 grenade launcher, he delivered highly accurate fire and directed the fire of his men and the armored vehicles against the hostile positions with such effectiveness that seven enemy soldiers were killed and the hostile fire silenced. After ensuring that all casualties were cared for and every man in his patrol accounted for, he then moved the Marines out of the dangerous area and returned to his base. Second

Lieutenant North's courage, superb leadership and unwavering devotion to duty in the face of great personal danger inspired all who observed him and were in keeping with the highest traditions of the Marine Corps and of the United States Naval Service."

The Combat Distinguishing Device is authorized.

FOR THE PRESIDENT

H.W. BUSE, JR.

*LIEUTENANT GENERAL, U.S. MARINE CORPS*
*COMMANDING GENERAL, FLEET MARINE FORCE, PACIFIC*

The President of the United States takes pleasure in presenting the SILVER STAR MEDAL to

SECOND LIEUTENANT
OLIVER L. NORTH
UNITED STATES MARINE CORPS

for service as set forth in the following

*CITATION:*

"For conspicuous gallantry and intrepidity in action while serving as Platoon Commander with Company K. Third Battalion, Third Marines, Third Marine Division in connection with combat operations against the enemy in the Republic of Vietnam. On 25 May 1969, while Company K was participating in Operation Virginia Ridge near the Demilitarized Zone, the lead platoon came under a heavy volume of machine gun and automatic weapons fire supported by rocket-propelled grenades, directional mines, and mortars. In the initial burst of fire, the platoon commander and point squad leader were seriously wounded. Realizing the need for immediate action, Second Lieutenant North rapidly maneuvered his Second Platoon through the lines of the beleaguered unit and personally initiated an aggressive assault against the North Vietnamese Army emplacement, the momentum of which forced the stunned hostile soldiers to withdraw to another hill and enabled the treatment and evacuation of Marine casualties. After regrouping his forces, he fearlessly led an attack on the enemy's new position, killing one soldier as his men closed with the enemy, and causing the North Vietnamese Army force to retreat to a previously prepared entrenchment on the ridgeline. Again reorganizing his men, Second Lieutenant North, with complete disregard for his own safety, assumed the foremost assault position and, seemingly oblivious to the intense machine gun fire impacting around him, led his men against the hostile position. As the tempo of the battle increased, casualties mounted, and his unit's ammunition supply became short. Unwilling to unnecessarily risk the lives of his men, he halted the attack and, repeatedly exposing himself to the heavy volume of fire delivered by the determined enemy soldiers, boldly directed the resupply of his platoon and the evacuation of the injured Marines. After skillfully adjusting fixed wing air strikes upon the North Vietnamese Army unit, Second Lieutenant North dauntlessly initiated a fourth assault by his wearied men. Calmly braving the intense fire of the tenacious hostile soldiers, he moved from one Marine to another, directing their fire and exhorting them to a last bold effort which, by his valorous perseverance, enabled his men to push the remainder of the North Vietnamese Army force from the ridgeline and to seize the objective. His heroic actions and vigorous efforts inspired all who observed him and contributed significantly to the defeat of the enemy. By his courage, dynamic leadership and unwavering devotion to duty in the face of grave personal danger, Second Lieutenant North upheld the highest traditions of the Marine Corps and of the United States Naval Service."

FOR THE PRESIDENT,

H.W. BUSE, JR.

*LIEUTENANT GENERAL, U.S. MARINE CORPS*
*COMMANDING GENERAL, FLEET MARINE FORCE, PACIFIC*

# Oliver L. North:
# A Chronology

**1943**

**October 7**     Oliver Laurence North is born in San Antonio, Texas, to Army Major Oliver Clay North and Ann Clancy North. By the late 1940s, the North family had returned to Philmont, New York, to join the textile business started by North's paternal grandfather, Oliver Laurence North. Larry is the oldest of four children.

**1957**

**September**     Larry North attends Christian Brothers Academy, Albany, New York, for his freshman year of high school. It is an Army-affiliated military school. North commutes from Philmont, where he went to grade school.

**1958**

**September**     Returns to public school at Ockawamick High School.

**1961**

**June**     Graduates from Ockawamick High School, voted the "best-looking" in his class of thirty-five seniors.

**September**    Enrolls at Brockport State College, a teachers' college near Rochester, New York, where he majors in English. Meets the son of the soccer coach at Annapolis.

**December**    Joins the Marine Platoon Leadership Corps, part of the Marine Corps Reserve.

**1962**

**July**    Takes basic training for Marine Reserves at Camp Lejeune, North Carolina.

**1963**

**June**    North begins his plebe year at the United States Naval Academy, Annapolis, Maryland. North completed two years of college at Brockport State. At 20, he is older than the other entering plebes of the Class of 1967.

**1964**

**February**    North and four Academy classmates are in an automobile accident near Corning, New York. One classmate is killed. North suffers a debilitating leg injury and is forced to leave Annapolis.

**September**    North returns to the Naval Academy and re-enters as a plebe. He also begins intramural boxing to maintain the conditioning begun after his car accident. He now expects to graduate with the Class of 1968.

**1965**

**November**    North plays in the Turkey Bowl, the sophomore–junior football game at the Naval Academy in spite of doctor's orders to avoid contact sports that might reinjure his leg.

**1967**

**February**    North fights James Webb, now the Secretary of Navy, for the 147-pound brigade championship, the Academy's top boxing title. He wins the three-round match by decision, then uses the film of the fight to persuade his superiors that he is fit enough to join the Marines.

**September**    North becomes commander of the Seventh Company, a leadership position that is highly competitive.

**1968**

**March**    Betsy Stuart goes on her first date with North. Introduced to him by his cousin, Stuart is working at a Washington, D.C., department store.

**June**    North is commissioned a second lieutenant in the Marine Corps on June 5. He graduates in the middle of his class.

**November**    North completes officer training at The Basic School, Quantico, Virginia. On the 13th, he and Betsy Stuart are married at the Memorial Chapel.

**December**    After a honeymoon cut short by his assignment to Vietnam, North leaves December 3 to become a platoon leader with K Company, Third Battalion, Third Marines, Third Marine Division. He serves eight months in I Corp, near the DMZ.

**1969**

**February**    North receives a Bronze Star for continuing to direct his platoon in spite of injuries received when thrown off a tank. He climbed back on the tank to retrieve the radio so he could call for air support.

**May**    North leads his Second Platoon into enemy fire to rescue a seriously wounded fellow platoon leader. The assault drives the NVA from a hill emplacement permitting the evacuation of injured Marines. North receives a Silver Star for this action. North, stunned by a mortar explosion, is pulled to safety by a corporal. North will later return to testify on behalf of the Marine who is accused of committing war atrocities.

**September**   Promoted to first lieutenant.

**November**   North leaves the Republic of Vietnam to return to The Basic School as an instructor of combat patrolling. He begins his rise in rank, spending over three years at Quantico.

## 1971

**May**   North and two fellow officers appear on William F. Buckley's television show, *Firing Line,* after writing the networks criticizing their coverage of the Vietnam War as unfair to American servicemen.

**July**   North is promoted to captain.

## 1973

**November**   Assigned to the Northern Training Area, North begins a year of duty in the rugged terrain of Okinawa, Japan. He runs a rigorous guerrilla warfare and survival training school.

**1974**

**December**     Returning to the United States, North spends twenty-one days at the Bethesda Naval Hospital. The subject of much speculation, he is said to be suffering from either emotional distress or physical exhaustion. Marine Corps officials say that North was released fit for duty.

**1975**

**January**     North begins a three-and-a-half year assignment at Marine Corps Headquarters near the Pentagon in Arlington, Virginia. As a manpower analyst, North attends to the personnel needs of an all-volunteer armed forces.

**1978**

**June**     A month before being promoted to major, North returns to teaching, calling on the skills honed at Quantico and Okinawa. He is assigned to Camp Lejeune, North Carolina, the main Marine amphibious warfare training center.

**1980**

**April**     North is with a Marine amphibious unit in the Mediterranean waiting to back up the ill-fated attempt to rescue the American hostages held at the U.S. Embassy in Tehran.

**July**     North is chosen for the Naval War College, Newport, Rhode Island. A paper that he writes on the recommissioning of battleships mothballed after World War II brings him to the attention of John Lehman. Secretary of Navy Lehman later is instrumental in bringing him to the National Security Council.

**1981**

**August**     North is appointed to the National Security Council. He is assigned to temporary duty to help lobby Congress on the sale of AWACs to the Saudis. The effort is led by then Major General Richard Secord, who had been with the Defense Department and goes on to become a covert operations specialist with North.

**1983**

**October 1**     North promoted to lieutenant colonel. That same month Robert McFarlane becomes National Security Advisor and gives North the job of liaison with the Contras in Nicaragua.

**1984**

**May**     North meets the leadership of the Contras at a meeting in Honduras. North tells them that in spite of the restrictive Boland Amendment, the Reagan Administration will continue to aid them. That becomes his principal responsibility.

**September**     North suggests to NSC director McFarlane that a private donor be found to replace a helicopter shot down by the Sandinistas in Nicaragua.

**1985**

**June**     TWA Flight 847 is hijacked in the Middle East, and one person, an American sailor, is murdered. North, in charge of the NSC's antiterrorist group, faces yet another frustrating terrorist incident. He establishes valuable intelligence ties with the Israelis during the incident.

**July**     North organizes a meeting at the Miami International Airport Hotel between Contra political director Adolfo Calero and now-private citizen Richard Secord. The all-night session marks the beginning of the covert arms resupply network that North will run for the next year and a half.

**October 7**     North's 42nd birthday

The *Achille Lauro* cruise ship is seized by Palestinian hijackers in the Mediterranean. In North's finest hour, the colonel masterminds a midair "Yamamoto," forcing the escaping hijackers' airplane down in Sicily, where they are arrested.

**1986**

**February**     North visits London and Germany to meet with Iranian arms dealers. He has been tasked with freeing the American hostages in Lebanon and believes that Iran can be persuaded to help free them.

**April**     The U.S. bombs Libya in retaliation for ordering the bombing of a West Berlin disco. North had spent weeks helping to plan the early morning raid.

**April**     North shows up on terrorist Abu Nidal's hit list.

**May**     North flies to Tehran with McFarlane, three other Americans and a planeload of arms for the Iranians. After five days of meetings with Iranian intermediaries, the Americans leave without resolving the hostage issue.

**July**     The Reverend Lawrence Jenco, a Beirut hostage, is released as a result of Iranian pressure on the hijackers. American intelligence confirms that the May delivery of arms made the difference.

**October**    A C-123K cargo plane is shot down by the Nicaraguans. The sole survivor is American Eugene Hasenfus, who says he has been helping to deliver arms for the United States Government.

500 TOW missiles are delivered to Iran as a result of recently concluded meetings between an American team led by North and an Iranian team supposedly representing a moderate faction in the Tehran government.

**November**    David Jacobsen is released as a result of the latest arms shipment.

A Lebanese magazine exposes the story of American arms sales to Iran.

After a tumultuous three weeks of nationwide press coverage and congressional pressure, North is forced to resign. Attorney General Meese says he might be subject to criminal prosecution for diverting Iranian arms funds to the Contras.

**December**    North takes the Fifth Amendment before a Senate Committee investigating the Iran-Contra Affair.

A special prosecutor is named to investigate

and prosecute possible criminal wrongdoing in the affair.

## 1987

**February**    The Tower Commission investigating the matter issues its report. It cites many failures in the way the Iran arms deals and Contra resupply operation were run and monitored by the NSC.

**May**    The Joint Committees of Congress begin their hearings. Colonel North appears for the first time on July 7. His testimony is aired by all three national television networks for each of the six days he appears. Overnight he becomes a national celebrity.